A Perfect Heart

My Story

John Healy

with Michelle O'Keeffe

Contents

This book is dedicated to my donor.
Thank you for saving my life

Acknowledgements

I always knew I had a book in me and very often, at different stages throughout my life, I promised to write it. This book has been written in conjunction with the therapy I went through before and after my transplant. My counsellor, Caroline has gently taken me to the depths within and gave me the courage to face the past I dreaded. It was with her help I found my strength again.

To put words on paper is not an easy task. More often than not, I got lost in the emotional exhaustion of trudging through memories that I thought were buried for good. I was kept in the story by my ghost writer, Michelle O'Keeffe. I am so thankful for her patience and understanding, even when faced with substantial rewrites. I am very grateful to her for helping me tell my story.

As a restaurant manager, you are only as good as your team. Undoubtedly, my support has been my friends. Throughout the years they have supported me emotionally, spiritually and at times financially. I would not have made it through the past five years without them. My friends, neighbours, colleagues and customers of the Four Seasons have been fantastic. They all know who they are.

My family have been through so much, especially in the past few years. I pray that we have seen the last of illness and hospitals and we can now move forward together in harmony and peace.

'That which does not kill us makes us stronger.'

Introduction

A searing pain shot up my arm and took hold of my chest. A strange feeling engulfed me and the colour drained from my face. I couldn't catch my breath. It was like the room was closing in on me. The pain was not like the experience of being cut or hit, it was an internal pain. The whole electrical system in my body was going into meltdown, like a robot malfunctioning. It felt weird, but it was a strangeness I knew. It was a heart attack. I couldn't believe it – I was having another heart attack. I was forty-four years of age and I was having my second heart attack.

Before having my first heart attack two years previously, I had been playing with fire, but my lifestyle had changed dramatically since then. I was healthier than I had ever been in my life after giving up my partying ways and I was eating healthy, exercising and had lost twenty kilos in weight. Not a drop of drink passed my lips any more and drugs were a thing of the past. My only vice left was my twenty-a-day cigarette habit. I was on the way to being fully fit and healthy. Giving up cigarettes was the last thing I had to do and I felt brilliant.

It was 9.50 AM on a cold November day in 2009. I was sitting on my black leather chair looking at the calming water of the canal from the massive window in my city centre apartment. I was feeling good. Later that day I was going to the Rutland Centre to pick up my medallion for eighteen months of sobriety.

I had a mug of coffee in one hand and a cigarette in the other when I suddenly got this pain in my chest. I thought it was maybe a muscle spasm or caused by anxiety, as I had experienced both since my first heart attack. But then the pain came again and I knew it was not anxiety, it was the real thing. After having experienced a heart attack before I knew exactly what was going on, and it was terrifying. I just sat there. I couldn't believe it. I couldn't believe it was happening again. I went and lay down on my bed and all I could think was that I couldn't do it.

I had been through hell in the last two years since my first heart attack, suffering from depression and anxiety. I had had suicidal tendencies over that time and had done a stint in rehab. I had just come through all that and now it was happening again. For a split second I considered not ringing anyone and just dying. I was doubled over in pain on my bed, grasping my phone in my hand and thinking maybe it would be better to just go now. But then the faces of my family and friends came into my mind and I knew I couldn't leave them – I didn't want to leave them. I called my neighbour and she rushed into my apartment and called an ambulance. I knew I had to get to hospital quickly. I grabbed my bag of medication and walked down the stairs and through the car park of the complex to the main road where the ambulance was waiting for me. I told the paramedics I was having a heart attack and I knew they didn't believe me as I was looking so healthy. I told them I had one before and handed them my bag of medication. I was put in the back of the ambulance, a monitor was strapped to me and I was in St Vincent's Hospital within five minutes.

The cardiologist, who had treated me before, was on the wards doing his rounds. He carried out a carotid angioplasty, which involved him making a surgical cut in my groin and inserting a catheter into my artery. A wire was passed through the catheter to the blockage and another catheter with a small balloon on the end was pushed in to the blockage and blown up to open up my artery. A stent was also inserted. A balloon was keeping me alive. It was touch and go for twenty-four hours. Fluid had built up on my lungs because of the heart failure and doctors thought I had pneumonia.

It was very different to my first heart attack. It was a much more traumatic experience and truly terrifying. There was a lot of damage done to my heart muscles the second time around. My first heart attack was not as forceful and the pain didn't last as long. This time I really believed I could die.

My first heart attack happened at midnight in that same leather chair, as I sat with my flatmate at the time, Elaine Normile. Despite being exhausted by the hectic Christmas season in the Four Seasons, where I worked as maître d', I was unable to go to bed as my mind was spinning out of control. It was our regular routine after work to sit into the early hours of the morning drinking mugs of tea, smoking cigarettes and eating pizza.

We had just returned home from Athlone, where we were recording *The Restaurant* for RTÉ, and all of a sudden I started to feel strange. I thought I was just stressed and tired so I said goodnight to Elaine and went in and lay on my bed. But I couldn't breathe so I went to open the window in my bedroom and I felt very weak. When a pain went down my arm I started to think I could be having a heart attack. The internal conversation in my brain went back and forth: 'You can't be having a heart attack', 'I am having a heart attack', 'You can't be having a heart attack, you are too young, you are too fabulous.' I went out to Elaine in the sitting room and told her to call an ambulance. Then I lost consciousness and when I came around I was on the ground bent over holding my shoulder and my arm. When I looked up there were two paramedics standing over me.

In St Vincent's hospital, doctors put IVs in both my arms, I was connected to an ECG and crash pads were used on me. It was very surreal and very scary. They gave me morphine and that just calmed me down completely and I felt like I was floating, like it was all happening to someone else. At 7.30 AM the next morning I was taken to the CAT lab, opened up and had stents inserted. The following day I was sitting up in the hospital bed. The serotonin level in my system must have increased because I never felt better. As I came down off the morphine, I became very emotional and depressed. But because of my experience of taking drugs, I knew I would get through the coming down period. And I recovered in no time; I was back working in the Four Seasons by Paddy's Day.

It took the second heart attack to stop me in my tracks. After my second hospitalisation, I went home to my parents' house in Kildare. It was just before Christmas and I felt vulnerable and scared. The morning after I got home I was lying in bed in my old bedroom in the family home and I had the strangest experience. As I lay there wide awake, the film of my life played before my eyes, each scene a vivid memory of my past. It was as if my memories were re-setting themselves after the heart attack. Events from my past came back to haunt me. There was the innocent seven-year-old boy, standing proudly in his Holy Communion outfit; me playing with my sisters in the strawberry fields at our parents' first house in Kilkenny; the faces of the men that repeatedly sexually abused me, the neighbour, the teacher, the family member. There was me as a flamboyant character at college with the girls I had once loved and hearts I had broken; the heady days of London, where I finally came out as being gay, my family's struggle to accept my sexuality; the parties in London and New York and the after effects of my hectic lifestyle. The film of my life showed the good days, but mainly it brought home the destruction and devastation I had lived through, and the things that went wrong.

It was a horror movie and I couldn't switch it off.

I lay in the bed with tears running down my face.

I

Childhood

*May I always remember that the power within me is far greater
than the fear before me.*

As a child, I could often be found sitting in the strawberry patch in our sprawling back garden in Goresbridge, Kilkenny with my older sister, Mairead and my baby sister, Mary. The sun scorching down, we crouched among the plants for hours munching on big, ripe strawberries as the juice ran down our chubby cheeks. Those strawberries were the most delicious we had ever tasted, and believing our parents were unaware of our pre-dinner feast made them all the sweeter. As we greedily picked them straight from the green foliage and stuffed them into our mouths, Mairead kept us mesmerised with magnificent stories of princes and princesses and great adventures.

My earliest childhood memory of the strawberry patch is having a row with Mary when I was four and she was only two-and-a-half. We were sitting together among the fruit and I was playing with one of my favourite toy trucks. Mary decided she wanted it and grabbed the truck out of my hands. I raced to the kitchen in tears, intent on reporting this great injustice to my mother. Always the diplomat and well used to our little squabbles, our mother insisted that we kiss and make up, explaining to us that our friendship was more important than any toy. We were too young to understand the life lesson but were immediately willing to be friends again. There is still a photograph in my parents' house of myself and Mary that day, hugging tightly and giving each other a big kiss. Every time I see that picture it triggers vivid memories of the fun the three of us had together.

Mairead, Mary and I were like the three amigos. We spent hours playing together in our back garden during the summer or in the garage when it was raining or cold. As we were all so close in age – Mairead was a year older than me and Mary a year-and-a-half younger – we were the best of pals. We loved being outside exploring; there was great freedom in the countryside and that sprawling garden in Goresbridge was a dream playground for us. We all had great imaginations and could occupy ourselves for hours after school and on those long summer days during the holidays. When the Aga Khan was on TV we would gather wood and broken branches, build makeshift fences and pretend to be horses gracefully navigating the obstacle course. It was serious business and it took great concentration to ensure our little legs did not knock over a fence, as Mairead kept score of our performance. When Wimbledon started we transformed our garden into a tennis court using rope for a net. The competition was fierce but in keeping with tradition, there was always time to gorge on strawberries during the well-earned set breaks!

One of our most treasured possessions was an old dress-up box, crammed with my mother's old dresses, high heel shoes, jackets and hats.

It was taken out often as we decided who we were going to be that day. The girls were always princesses, pulling on oversized dresses that swept the floor and shoes they could barely hobble around in. Sometimes I was a pirate, but mostly I liked to dress up as a gentleman, with a suit jacket down to my knees and a top hat that constantly slipped over my eyes. However, impaired vision and a clumsy costume was no match for a brave and gallant knight intent on rescuing princesses from the clutches of evil monsters, and we played our parts with gusto.

Once I had rescued the princesses and we were getting peckish, we climbed through the fence to our next-door neighbour, Mrs Bridge. She was a lovely old lady who doted on us – she always had a treat ready for us when we found are way into her house. Her back door was routinely unlocked and we would march straight into her kitchen. She would pretend she didn't know who we were, much to our delight. Of course, we adventurers had travelled a long way and were very hungry. We clambered onto chairs around her big table and she fed us glasses of ice-cold milk and biscuits as we told her about the great adventures and battles we had just returned from.

The only place in our garden that was strictly out of bounds was the river that ran through the bottom of it. It was the River Borrow, and our parents drilled into us how dangerous it was. We knew we were banned from going anywhere near it on our own, and we never did. At the weekends, our father would take us down to the water, which was a real treat. Our father, Jeremiah – everyone called him Jerry – worked in Connolly's Mills. We all adored him and loved our time spent with him at weekends. My mother, Nuala, was the disciplinarian. She was well able to handle us and was strict, but fair. There was never a call for 'wait until your father gets home'; my mother could more than keep us in line on her own! We were good, well-mannered children. Mischievous maybe, but we always said please and thank you. On Saturdays, armed with fishing nets, we marched delightedly beside our father down to the river. I was all about the tadpoles. They were my little fascination. On many occasions my mother came across jam jars under my bed – each one covered in cling film, pierced with airholes and full to the brim with tadpoles. I loved watching them grow and then releasing the frogs.

We had dinner around the table as a family every day, even if sometimes my mother had a job trying to get us indoors to eat. There were sometimes tears when we were dragged away from our game, especially if I was interrupted on the verge of rescuing the princesses. There was a vegetable patch in our garden with potatoes, carrots, cabbage, lettuce and scallions, which were picked fresh every day. My mother is a brilliant cook. There was great fun around the table as our parents listened to us excitedly telling them about what we had got up to that day. Our home was always full of laughter and love.

Christmas in our house was magical. Determined to avoid disappointment, I was very precise when it came to my wish list and spent weeks every year writing and re-writing my letter to Santa Claus. On Christmas Eve we sat around the radio listening to hear if Santa had left the North Pole. There was always a lot of impatient shushing if one of my sisters dared speak before I discovered Santa's location. Milk and carrots were dutifully left on the kitchen table for the reindeers, while Santa was presented with biscuits, Snack bars, and either whiskey or Guinness, depending on his preferred tipple at the time. The two girls shared a room and I had my own. As I lay in bed, bubbling over with excitement, I was convinced I heard the reindeers' hooves on our roof. I would scurry into the girls' room to see if they had heard it too, which they obviously always had! One of my favourite Christmases was 1968 when we woke up to find three bicycles under the tree. At 5 AM we rode our bicycles up and down the hallway, squealing with delight.

Every year, after opening presents, we put on our new Christmas clothes and went to our grandparents, Paddy and Margaret Brennan's, for dinner. We sat down to a feast. Their house was always full of people and after dinner our uncles, aunts and cousins would arrive laden with gifts. It was a mad house, but a happy one, with children full of lemonade racing around, giddy with excitement.

I loved being in my granny and grandfather's house, which was on the other side of Kilkenny to our home in Goresbridge. They owned a 200-acre farm with cows, chickens, pigs, dogs and cats, and I spent many weekends there following the farmers around thinking I was a great help. Every day at exactly 1 PM my grandmother fed as many as fourteen workmen a three-course dinner; it often seemed as if her cooker was covered in pots of spuds and homemade vegetable soup for weeks on end. They came from the fields, marched into the house in their muddy boots and squeezed around the big table. The conversation was always about the weather, crops and animals. There was also talk about which neighbour drank a whiskey-too-many on Friday night in the local pub, or whose son or daughter was getting married.

I loved my grandparents' house and I continued to spend holidays there after we had moved to Naas. Every time I had a break from school

– Christmas, Easter, the summer – I wanted to be on my grandparents' farm. Every morning I got up at 5 AM and had a hearty breakfast before heading out with my grandfather to milk the cows. It was here, as a twelve-year-old boy, that I first learnt to drive – a tractor. There was not much I could wreck on the farm's open ground, but I still managed to plough into an open gate. I thought I had got the hang of driving but clearly not. I was moving at a snail's pace and aiming to get out of the field, but as I manoeuvred the tractor, I lost control of the steering and went straight into the gate. My grandfather just couldn't figure out how I had managed to find something to crash into, but I did. I have wonderful memories of those days spent on the farm and I loved spending time with my grandparents, but I never wanted to be a farmer; even then I knew it was not glamorous enough for me.

Goresbridge was an idyllic, picturesque village, and we loved going there with our mother when she did her shopping. It was a close-knit community and she seemed to know everyone in the village, stopping every few yards to chat. But when I was seven years old my father got a job in Bord na Móna and we moved to Naas. It was an August Bank Holiday weekend when all our belongings were loaded into a lorry. I was not sad or upset about leaving; I was too excited about the whole thing. To a chorus of 'are we there yet?' from me and my sisters, we travelled up in the car behind the truck carrying our beds, tables, chairs, drawers and sofa. The journey only took an hour and a half but it felt like we had been driving for hours, like we were going to a new, exotic land. I was very impressed when we did arrive. It was a two-storey house in a new development, so I thought it was a mansion. There was even a balcony.

The beds wouldn't fit through the front door and I couldn't stop laughing as I watched my father and uncles murmuring under their breath, struggling to hoist the beds through the balcony, as my mother directed operations from the ground.

There were loads of kids in the area and they all came over, curious about what was going on and who we were. A little girl came across the road dressed like a bumblebee in a vivid yellow and black striped jumper. Her name was Fiona Healy and she became my sister Mary's best friend. We were immediately accepted into the gang and spent our days racing around on our choppers. There was always someone knocking on the door to ask if we could come out to play and we would spend hours together building castles and forts. At one end of the road there was a creepy old house, which every child in the neighbourhood was terrified to go near – it was universally agreed by the gang to be haunted. Despite this, we were always daring each other to go into it and one day a group of us decided to explore the house and try to catch a glimpse of the ghosts.

We walked up to the front garden. I was petrified, but there was no way I was going to be the first one to chicken out. We crept into the dilapidated house clutching our torches, and made our way into one of the dusty rooms. Sitting in a circle, we began telling ghost stories. As I focused the light from the torch on my face for dramatic effect, the tension got too much for two of the younger girls, Orla and Grainne Byrne, and they ran screaming out of the house and back to their mammy. The next day as I sat watching TV there was a knock on the door; it was Mrs Byrne and she needed to talk to Mrs Healy about John.

I heard her mention sleepless nights and nightmares and I knew I was in trouble. I quickly worked out a plan of action – deny I was the storyteller and blame someone else. It worked.

Despite this little victory, it became increasingly difficult to get away with much when my mother got a job in the children's clothes shop in town, Nippers, which she eventually bought. It was the most popular children's clothes shop in the area and most kids were dressed out of it, but it became a great centre for gossip as well. Every mother in the area went to Nuala's shop, so she heard all the stories about the mischief we got up to. She knew everyone and everyone knew her. She would arrive home in the evenings and tell me where I had been and what I had done the day before. However, there was a plus side – tickets for *Joseph and the Amazing Technicolour Dreamcoat* performed in Goffs were sold in my mother's shop. I loved musicals, and this one was my favourite. Not very cool for a young boy, but I didn't care. I was obsessed with the show and infatuated with Tony Kenny, who played Joseph. I had posters of him on my bedroom wall, which was surely a sign of things to come. Because my mother sold the tickets, Mary, Mairead and I saw the show ten times, each time with front-row seats. We were fanatics; we knew every word and sang along to the whole show. We were word-perfect, if not exactly note-perfect. We spent hours at home practising the show in our bedroom and putting performances on for our parents, and anyone else who would listen. I, of course, got the starring role as Joseph. I was only fabulous.

I started in the CBS primary school in Naas and Mary and Mairead went to the Presentation Convent. I was in second class and my teacher was Mr McGovern. He was a lovely man and I loved school. All my friends from the area went to the same school and we had great fun. I loved sport and enjoyed playing tennis and football at lunchtime. I was even on the school rugby team.

My pals and I often travelled to school together on our bikes. One day I was racing my neighbours Paul and Tommy Sheehan home and, intent on victory, I took a short cut through a field. Not thinking, I flew out the gate and onto the road. Before I knew what was happening a car hit me and I was thrown up into the air; I smacked onto the bonnet and landed on the road with a bang. There was nothing the shocked driver could have done – I came out of nowhere. The horrified motorist rang an ambulance as Paul cycled as fast as he could to my house to get my mother. When I came around and opened my eyes, the first thing I saw was my mother's red mini coming towards me. The pain was out of this world as my mother spoke to me softly and caressed my head, her face ashen white. My leg was bent behind me. Fortunately, the local doctor was passing and stopped. She rolled up my school jumper, put it between my legs and tied them together with my tie.

I remember the loud siren of the ambulance as my mother travelled with me, holding my hand the whole time. I felt every bump in the road and the pain consumed me. I was taken to Crumlin Children's Hospital where the doctors told my mother I had broken my fibula in two places. I was too small to put my leg in plaster so it was put in a splint and traction, but my leg wasn't healing and continued to swell, so a week later a pin was put through my shin bone and weights were used to level out my leg. I was in that hospital bed for three months. I could not move and spent most of the time crying; the pain was horrendous. My mother drove up to the hospital every day, sometimes twice a day. But every hour dragged as I lay there staring at the ceiling. I had a little orange radio and I listened to Gay Byrne and Larry Googan but I was lonely and afraid and missed playing with my friends. When eventually I got to go home I was very weak and withdrawn and spent months going to a physiotherapist to try and regain the strength in my muscles. It was a difficult, lengthy process and I had no interest in sports after the accident. But I got strong again and was delighted to finally be back out playing with my friends and going on adventures.

****

Looking back on my childhood, those years seem almost idyllic. And for much of that time I was a happy and contented child. But I had a dark secret that I had kept hidden from my parents and my friends. I was being abused.

The first time a man sexually abused me I was eight years old. Even at such a young age, I knew something terrible was happening to me. I couldn't understand why this person was doing such horrible things; it felt wrong and I was horrified. I don't remember being afraid but I did feel that what this person was doing to me was not right. It was very confusing.

As the abuse continued, I began to adapt and accept that what was happening was normal. I started to believe that the affection he showed me was worth the price I was paying. He never threatened me to make sure I didn't tell my parents, I don't know why. Once I was abused the first time I changed forever. I began to look for affection, affirmation of love and acceptance through sex. The purity and innocence of my childhood was gone and I could no longer differentiate between love and sex. I was too young to know what sex was, but I saw it as a sign someone cared about me.

There were five men who abused me consecutively over a long period of time. I was a child, I didn't understand what was happening, and these adults took advantage of that. It was a secret life that only my abusers and I knew about.

By the time I was due to start secondary school, at Newbridge College, it seemed like a way out for me, a place I could escape the abuse for good. Boarding school was the perfect place to free myself – a haven where I could be safe. As there was no uniform at the school, my mother took me shopping and bought me all the latest trendy clothes: Levi jeans and flared corduroys. I wanted a pair of cowboy boots to finish off my new ensemble, but I settled for clogs. My mother meticulously stitched labels with my name onto my clothes and I packed my suitcase. I rocked up to the school feeling like a king. There was a certain independence with going to a boarding school, I felt grown up, even though I was only twelve years old. I felt free.

From the outset, I loved Newbridge College: the camaraderie among the boys, getting to have breakfast, lunch and dinner with my friends, the novelty of moving to a different classroom for every subject. There was a playroom with a pool table and we would steal from the tuck shop to have extra sweets and biscuits to eat in the dorm at night. It was like one big sleepover and I was in my element. I was part of a gang; I belonged. When the lights went off, you could hear homesick boys sobbing into their pillows as the rest of us giggled. I was happy to have settled in so well.

The carefree fun didn't last, however. A month after I started at the school, the headmaster, Fr Vincent Mercer, came into the dorm and sexually abused me. I couldn't believe it. He was a priest, a religious man who prayed and taught us about God. But here he was, with his big red face and groping hands fumbling under my bed sheets. I was frozen with shock and humiliation. My friends were lying in beds next to me and they could hear what was happening. The lads I hung around with were listening to me being abused. I was overcome with embarrassment and shame.

But I was not his only victim. Once the lights were turned off, Fr Mercer paced slowly around the dark dormitory, deciding which schoolboy he wanted that night. If it was not me, I knew it was one of my friends. The next morning at breakfast we always acted like nothing had happened – we never spoke about it and continued on as normal. But every night as I lay in my bed I listened with dread as his slow, loud footsteps echoed down the hall, the large crucifix clanging against the wrought iron beds as it swung from his waist. Frozen in fear and panic, I lay still, pretending to be asleep, praying the dull sound of his footsteps and the banging of the cross would not stop at my bed. I lay in silence, the bedclothes pulled up to my neck and my elbows pinning the blankets to the mattress. I lay wishing I could protect myself from his evil touch and heavy breath on my face.

Fr Mercer preyed on our vulnerability, using the power of his authority to exploit and abuse us. Nobody knew what to do. I was too ashamed and afraid to say out loud what was happening to me. It was my friend who finally broke down and told his father about the abuse he was suffering. His father contacted my parents and told them what was happening at school. When my father rang and asked if it was true, I finally broke my silence and told him everything.

Relief washed over me as I sat at the bottom of the stairs in the front hall of the school, waiting for my father to collect me. When I got home there was a conversation around the kitchen table about the abuse. Once I started talking everything came flooding out. I told them about all the years of sexual abuse and the people that did it. It was very difficult for me to tell them the vile things that had been done to me and it was heartbreaking for them to hear it. I don't think my parents knew how to cope with it. They just didn't know what to do. People's mentality in Ireland at that time was to sweep abuse under the carpet and just get on with it, and that is exactly what we did. I was withdrawn from Newbridge College. It was not spoken about again for a very long time.

The abuse I experienced at the hands of Fr Mercer had the most damaging psychological affect on me. He used the institutional power given to him by the Church in order to hide his evil, vile acts of abuse. At that time in Ireland nobody questioned the clergy and Fr Mercer used this control to do as he wished to me and other schoolboys. Parents trusted him to look after and protect their sons and he abused that trust. I later learned that Fr Mercer had told my parents when I first started Newbridge College that if they gave him a boy, he would give them back a man. He did exactly as he promised.

It was not until many years later that justice was done and Fr Mercer was made to pay for what he did. One day in 2001, I got a phone call from my old school friend who had first told his parents about the abuse. He now lived in New York and had recently started trying to confront and deal with the abuse he had suffered as a child. Part of his journey was to come back to Ireland and confront what Fr Mercer had done and ensure he was punished. He went to the dean of Newbridge College and told him the unthinkable things that were done to him while in their care. He was asked had anyone else been abused by Fr Mercer and he told him there had. He rang me and asked if I wanted to come forward and I agreed. I then met with the head of the Provincialate Dominican Order and told him everything. I was sent to a child sex therapist for a year, which they paid for, and a file was sent to the office of the Director of Public Prosecutions.

On 1 March 2005, Fr Vincent Mercer appeared in Naas Circuit Criminal Court. He was given a three-year suspended sentence for sexually abusing six schoolboys in Newbridge College, as well as two more boys at a holiday camp in Cork between 1970 and 1977. At the time of sentencing, Judge Raymond Groake said that Fr Mercer had carried out a 'reign of terror' in abusing vulnerable first- and second-year students. I didn't go to court that day; I didn't feel the need to face the priest or look him in the eyes. It was a profoundly confusing time. Although I hated that man for what he had done to me and how the abuse had affected my life, but I also felt sorry for him. An old man being forced to face the vile things he had done to children. He is a paedophile; he knew that what he was doing was horrific, but it was like he couldn't help himself. I can almost pity that compulsion in him. But

I cannot forgive him. When I am around my sister's and friends' kids, I look at them and I cannot understand how anyone could harm them. Fr Mercer disgusts me, but I refuse to let him consume any more of my life.

It became increasingly difficult to hide from the haunting images of abuse that preoccupied my mind as I entered my teens. I felt that the only thing I could do to protect myself from the hurt and pain was to bury it. I was terrified people would see the broken, scared child within me, so I created a personality, like armour, to protect myself. I became the joker. I became convinced that by keeping those dark demons buried deep inside, and ensuring no-one around me even knew they existed, I would somehow be healed. I became very introverted sexually. There were no girlfriends, or boyfriends; I couldn't trust anybody enough to let them know the real me.

2

College Years

*How hurtful it can be to deny one's true self and live a life of
lies just to appease others.*

– June Ahern

It was such a relief to be taken out of Newbridge College, away from Fr
Mercer's grasp. My parents gave me the option of going to Clongowes
Wood College or Clane secondary school and I knew straight away
where I wanted to be. There was no way I was going to another boarding
school. At that stage, I needed the security of knowing that whatever
happened, I could be at home with my family at the end of each day. The
school in Clane provided this comfort. I wasn't even put off by the
horrendous uniform of grey trousers and jumper, brown shirt and green
tie. It was far from fashionable – the brown shirt particularly offended
me – but I was prepared to put it on every morning if it meant going
home every night. I was not, however, prepared to let my style go
completely out the window, and I pushed the uniform code right to its
limits, swapping the grey trousers for cords and wearing my white
leather shoes whenever I thought I could get away with it.

I joined the first year class in Clane just after Halloween. I travelled on the 8.20 AM CIE bus to school every morning – or that was the plan anyway. More often than not I missed the bus and would end up hitching to school. Attending Clane was a very different experience to my time spent at Newbridge, the biggest change being that I was now surrounded by girls. Clane was a mixed-sex school and the new female company delighted me. Of course, I probably would have been even more excited about having girls in my class if I had had any interest whatsoever in having a girlfriend, but even with teenage hormones racing around my body I knew I was not attracted to girls, either romantically or sexually. Despite this, I was more comfortable around girls and Noleen Henessey and Sheila Murphy became two of my best pals. We were inseparable and full of devilment and loved nothing more than sitting down the back of the classroom having a giggle about what the teacher was wearing. Considering we were all dressed in brown shirts and green ties, we were in no position to judge, but it kept us entertained nonetheless!

I took great pride in being the joker of the class, always hoping I could get the class to erupt into laughter at one of my cheeky one-liners. The teachers couldn't but like me and I always managed to win them over with charm when it counted most, so I rarely got into serious trouble. That is, except when I was in second year and I got caught smoking down the end of the school field by the big tree. It was lunchtime and I headed down to hang out with a couple of friends – the big tree was the cool place to be. A packet of cigarettes was produced and I gave it my best shot, even though I nearly turned green puffing away on the cigarette. However, I got even sicker when I saw a teacher heading towards us and we were all marched to the principal's office. There was major drama and I was suspended for a week. My parents banished me to my bedroom. I think they punished me because they felt they should, but after everything I had been through that year, this was not taken too seriously. They feigned anger.

I never mitched from school because to be honest, I liked being there; it was where my friends were. I didn't do any science subjects but enjoyed Maths and English, and adored Home Economics. I was one of only two boys in the class, but I loved cooking and was a dab hand in the kitchen. Baking was my forte; my Christmas cake won first prize at the school two years running. I was the teacher's pet in that class as I was eager to learn, but when it came to the rest of my classes I had very little interest. I was an intelligent kid and my grades were not bad, but they could have been a lot better. I was too busy being the class clown, hiding from the memories of the abuse. Coming up to the Junior Certificate my parents must have thought I was extremely diligent, spending hours in my bedroom. The perception was that I was studying hard for my exams. The reality was I was listening to the radio, drawing pictures and practicing my moves for the roller disco.

We were all about the roller disco held in Behan's Ballroom in Clane every Wednesday, Friday and Saturday night. It was a big thing at the weekends and everyone from my year attended religiously. The whole week was spent discussing whose parents were giving us a lift that weekend, who was picking us up and most importantly what we were going to wear. My favourite outfit for the roller disco was a white shirt buttoned down the side with shiny gold buttons, a bolero and light blue trousers that were very baggy. I had a Spandau Ballet-style haircut and considered myself a New Romantic, without the makeup; I was not adventurous enough for eyeliner in Clane. I was a vision of fashion and fabulousness on rollerblades. It was not just simply skating around to music; there were twists, spins and fancy footwork to master, and the faster you could go the better. Plenty of innocent romances began on the floor of the roller disco. Time was spent eyeing up the opposite sex, getting your friend to ask someone out and sneaking off for a kiss. I was very involved in the complicated matchmaking manoeuvres but I had no interest in it for myself. I knew I was gay but I was far from ready to admit it to anyone. I was more interested in showing off my moves and setting up my friends with the boys they fancied.

In fifth and sixth year the roller disco was replaced with house parties. There was a bash one night in Clane that all my school friends were going to. There was no way I could miss it, even if my parents disagreed, so I climbed out my bedroom window with a bag of cans and managed to get my bike out of the garage quietly enough for my parents to remain oblivious to my plan. The sheer determination to make sure I was at that party spurred me on as I cycled the six miles to Clane. The party was in my mate's house, whose parents were away for the weekend. When I got there we just sat around drinking our cans and listening to Fleetwood Mac, Bob Dylan and Neil Young. By the end of the night we had solved all the world's problems. It was all great until, in the early hours of the morning and after several beers, the cold reality hit me that I had to cycle that long journey home before my parents realised I was gone. It was a very sobering thought. I climbed onto the bike, feeling far from energetic and a little unsteady on my feet. Somehow, despite a few wobbles on the bike, I managed to make the journey back safely. I didn't get caught by my parents but nonetheless decided that cycling to parties was not for me! I certainly was not giving up on the parties, just on my means of transport to them.

I was great pals with Trish and Elaine, who both lived in Naas and were outrageous young women. They knew how to party and so did I. As we were usually getting picked up by one of our parents, we couldn't get too drunk. There was many a night we climbed into the car chewing gum to hide the smell of alcohol, desperately trying to act stone-cold sober but getting a fit of giggles at the ridiculous stories we were telling each other. We were definitely not fooling our parents that we were on lemonade all night.

There was no knuckling down to study in sixth year for me; I was just too busy having fun to spend my days with my head stuck in a book. I really didn't care about my Leaving Certificate. Trish, Elaine and I were having a ball and studying didn't appeal to me one little bit. My mother was very sick at the time. She had had a hysterectomy and there were complications in her recovery. Normally the person who kept us all in line, making us do our homework and study, my mother was too ill at that stage to keep control so there was not as much structure at home, and I took full advantage.

The Leaving Certificate was like a bad nightmare. I sat in the school hall convincing myself that by some miracle I was going to be able to answer the questions. But as I turned over the papers for every subject, frantically scanning the questions, I realised how little I knew. But not knowing the right answers didn't stop me from giving the papers a go; in every exam I tried to bluff, writing the most ridiculous thing that came into my head, hoping that some information had gone in by osmosis. It hadn't. When the day came to collect my results, I was so nervous I took a Valium to calm myself down. Elaine came with me for moral support, and we would usually be chattering away on the back of the bus the whole way to Clane, but this time I didn't utter a word. When I got to the school I opened the brown envelope and discovered what deep down I already knew – I had failed the Leaving Certificate in spectacular form. It was no real surprise to me, or anyone else, that I failed. But somehow I still thought I might have fluked it and impressed the examiners with the astounding bullshit I had come up with. My plan had failed. My mother was in hospital and my father at work so Elaine and I headed into Dublin city to meet the rest of our friends. We met up in the Dandelion Market, which was a cool place to hang out. We spent hours drinking take-away coffees and smoking cigarettes. Once I had gotten over the humiliation of failing I went home to face the music. I broke the news to my father, who in turn told my mother. They had not been expecting great things from my results but they were terribly disappointed and angry.

Around this time I became quite rebellious. One night, while walking home from the pub, a man in his thirties stopped his van and pretended he was looking for directions. I naïvely got into the van with him and one thing led to another. We were in the back of his van in a very compromising position when a blinding light shone in through the window. A garda was peering in at us and I was arrested. The sergeant in the local station knew me and rang my father. I was terrified and ashamed that my father had been told what I had done. Homosexuality was not even legal in Ireland at the time; and here I was sitting in a garda station after being caught in a sexual act with a man. My father was a well-known person in the area and very well respected. I am sure he was both horrified and mortified by the incident, and I felt guilty and ashamed for making him feel like that. The seven silent minutes in the car as we drove home were the most awkward of my life. But my father didn't say a word to me and the incident was never spoken of again.

After that it was decided by my parents that there was no way I was spending the whole summer partying. They were fully aware of my wild streak and were determined to keep it in check as best they could. I was sent to work with my father so that he could keep an eye on me. So that summer I spent three months working at Spread Ireland Ltd, which was a small-scale Bord na Móna, and had its own bog. It was a wholesaler for the gardening industry, selling everything from fertiliser to garden tools. My father was the managing director of the company and my job was in the warehouse, preparing orders for delivery. I was seventeen years old and really didn't give a damn about what I was going to do with my life. But one thing was certain: I didn't want to be working there for the summer. I wanted to be having fun with my friends. I was a stroppy teenager and horrible to my father. Every time he gave me instructions I was hostile and snappy towards him. He was very well respected in the business and having me act so petulantly must have been embarrassing.

I began to drink quite a lot; I went to the pub every night and tried to work every day, but I was too hungover to function. To say my dad was not impressed would be a massive understatement. It was definitely not a good working relationship. We are very similar, like two peas in a pod, which did not work in our favour when we were living in the same house and working together every day. It was a recipe for disaster and it was a particularly tense summer in our house.

I may not have known what I wanted to do, but I quickly realised what I didn't. It was near the end of that summer that I was arrested after being discovered in the back of a van with an older man. After that, my parents decided that if I was not going to find direction in my life, then they were going to find it for me. My mother told me that the money I had saved from working was going to be put to good use. There were no options given, I was informed I was going to the Institute of Education to repeat my Leaving Certificate and I was covering the cost of the fee. It was £800 for the year, which was a lot of money. I had already saved £500 so I was told I had to work until the beginning of term to make up the difference. Having let my parents down and now determined to make them proud again, I agreed. I was also encouraged by the fact that I hated the job I was doing and the only way I could get out of it was by re-sitting my Leaving Certificate.

Going to the Institute felt like going to university, and was a real eye-opener for me. I had always struggled with instruction and resisted how authoritarian school had been in Clane. But this was a completely new experience. At the Institute it was up to me to decide whether to go to class, and a lot of the teachers were more like lecturers, with a very different style of teaching. I took responsibility for myself and began to feel like a college student. I was now paying for my own education and I was not going to waste it this time round. I didn't have a school bag any more, I had a satchel and I felt very grown up. I did something I had never tried before: I studied. I attended study groups after school and spent hours at the weekends in the UCD library in Earlsfort Terrace pouring over books and writing essays. But it was not all work; there was a great social life attached to the Institute and we spent plenty of time in the Berni Inn at the bottom of Grafton Street. But even if the craic was good on a Friday after class, I always got the bus home after a couple of pints to make sure I was fit to study the next day. I had a good social life but I now took my study very seriously.

To sit the Leaving Certificate we went to Clongowes College. It was a very different experience the second time. When I turned the papers over I knew the answers. The results were posted to my house and as I opened the envelope I was desperately hoping that I would be happy with what I read. I got four honours and was delighted with myself. As I headed to town to the Berni Inn to celebrate with my friends I beamed with pride; I had set out to achieve something and I had done it.

With exams out of the way, I hatched a plan to ensure I would not be spending the summer working with my father again. I just couldn't face being stuck in that warehouse again. My parents' friend James Keogh owned the Lord Bagenal Inn in Leighlinbridge, County Carlow and he gave me a job. I had a lot of relatives in the area so I packed my bags and went to live with my aunt Angela Kelly and her husband Michael, who owned a big farm and haulage business. Angela was my young, cool aunt and I enjoyed living with them. They hardly ever saw me, however, as I worked eighty-hour weeks and usually just slept and ate on my days off. I started off as a lounge waiter, proved myself very quickly and was trained behind the bar. I worked very hard and adored it. I thrived on the hectic atmosphere – the speed of the job, the non-stop pressure and the craic. It was a real adrenalin rush. I got on great with the staff and the customers all loved me. It came natural to me to be able to serve drinks efficiently at a bar that was five rows deep and still manage to smile and chat to the customers at the same time. I worked from 11 AM to 1 AM every day with a couple of hours off in the afternoon. The split shifts didn't even bother me – during my break I either went for a walk after my lunch, or sat down by the river in Loughlinstown and ate my sandwiches.

That summer I found my niche. I cut down on drinking, got myself together and began to mature. I quickly decided I wanted a career in the hospitality industry and although my mother tried to discourage me, knowing how difficult a job it was and the long unsociable hours I would be expected to work, my mind was made up. I applied to study Hotel Management and Business at the DIT on Cathal Brugha Street. From the moment I made the decision, that course was all I wanted. There was simply nothing else that would do; there was no second choice or back-up plan for me, it was hotel management or nothing.

To my horror I didn't get a place on the course. I couldn't believe it. I was being denied something I knew I was meant to be doing. The second- and third-round offers came and went and still I didn't get a place. I was on a waiting list but my chances of being accepted at that stage were slim. But I was determined. The poor admissions officer in the college was Brendan Keyes and I phoned him almost daily for about four weeks. I was like a thorn in his side, constantly bombarding him with the same litany of questions – Where am I on the list now? Are there many people in front of me? Has anyone dropped out yet? What are my chances of getting on the course? I informed him I couldn't wait another year to get onto the course and assured him that I was going to persist until they let me in. It was September and the college had already started a week previously but there was no way I was giving up. In the end, Mr Keyes just got so sick of me that he got me a place on the course just so the calls would stop. I started college two weeks later.

On my first day I walked into one of the college buildings near Sheriff Street. I had never been in that part of town before; I preferred to keep in the radius of Brown Thomas. I felt a bit anxious as everyone else in the class had a head start on me and had already formed friendships. However, I waltzed into the science lab and just started chatting. I had learned over the years how to hide my fears but my classmates were a great bunch of people and before I knew it I was running the social club and involved in every society that involved partying.

I lived at home for the first year of college and travelled up and down from Naas on the bus. There were nights when I stayed with friends in town, but very rarely in the first year. I got a job as a waiter in Lawlors Hotel in Naas and worked every Friday and Saturday night, often Saturday lunch and Sunday lunch and sometimes Sunday night. I knew all the customers so it was great fun and because I regularly worked five shifts at the weekend, I had enough money to survive at college during the week.

I had made a vow to support myself. I had previously screwed everything up but I promised my parents that if they paid my college fees, I would handle the rest. But I still managed to have fun. The Welcome Inn on Parnell Street, which was just around the corner from the college, became our local. It was a haven for students and no matter what time you went in, day or night, there were always groups sitting around talking excitingly over pints. We headed there between lectures – a lecture, then the pub, and back to college. It was a great place. Not only did they have beer, they had the best toasted sandwiches in the city. A few beers in the middle of the day and half of us would be drunk and have to go home. I loved first year; I had great fun but I still did the work expected of me and got through my exams no problem.

Around that time, I started getting the travel bug and wanted to spend my three months off during the summer in a different country. I went to stay with my father's brother Eddie and his wife Georgette in Canada. I wanted to see the world and this seemed like a good place to start. I loved Toronto, indeed the whole feeling of being in North America. It was TV land to me, just so exciting. My aunt and uncle had a pool in their back garden, which seemed outrageously exotic and glamorous to me at the time. I was similarly impressed with my cousins and their friends' lifestyle. They seemed effortlessly cool, hanging out in diners and going to pool parties – a far cry from my student life spent in the Welcome Inn on Parnell Street. My uncle had secured me a visa to work with him in his electronics company, but of course I didn't want to work for him; I wanted a job in a hotel. I made him traipse around Toronto in the searing heat with me to all the places he socialised in to try and get me a job. I stood in my little suit in hotels, bars and restaurants as he talked me up, willing someone to give me work. But they couldn't hire me because of my visa restrictions, which stated that I had to work for my uncle, so there was nothing we could do. Despite my (and my uncle's) best efforts, I ended up in a warehouse, spending my days driving a forklift, moving big sheets of copper from one place to another. It was far from stylish and definitely not glamorous enough for me; I wanted to be running around a hotel charming customers.

I obviously wasn't cut out for warehouse work and my uncle soon discovered I was not to be trusted with a forklift. The outside door of the warehouse was higher than the inside door, which I hadn't realised at the time, and one day as I manoeuvred into the building with the forks up, I got caught on the inside door and pulled down the wall attached to it. The whole wall came crashing down. My cousin was sitting on a chair beside it but jumped out of the way just in time – the chair he was sitting on was completely demolished. After that near-death incident I was almost sent home, not surprisingly, but instead they decided working in a warehouse was not for me and my aunt took me on a road trip to tour Canada instead. I have never worked in a warehouse since.

My aunt Georgette hired a car and drove me and my cousin Darren to Ottawa and Montreal. It was a brilliant adventure; I loved every minute of it. We drove for hours chatting and singing; stopping at road-side diners for lunch. We stayed in Holiday Inns and made our plans as we went, which I thought was great. I fell in love with Montreal, it was so bohemian. We stayed with Georgette's brother but Darren and I spent a lot of time with his cousin Jeoff, who was slightly older than me, in his early twenties, and had his own apartment. He was a typical college student and I was slightly infatuated with him. We spent time hanging out with him in his place, drinking beers. He was into live music and rock bands and took us to a couple of gigs with his friends in very trendy underground bars. Jeoff had his own place, his own car and seemed to be able to do his own thing. He had a lot of freedom and I was hugely impressed; still relatively young and naïve, I was taken in by the way he lived and the bright lights of Montreal. After five days we travelled back by train and shortly afterwards I returned to Ireland.

Having seen how much fun Jeoff and his friends had living on their own, I decided I wanted a taste of that independence and moved to Dublin for my second year of college. My sister Mary had just finished her Leaving Certificate so we decided to get a flat together. I even had a girlfriend at the time. She was Mary's friend and I had met her in Naas. All my friends had girlfriends so it felt like the right thing to do and I wanted to conform and fit in with my peers. My girlfriend even moved into the flat with me and Mary. It was a little garden flat on Synge Street; I had my own room and the two girls shared another. It was riddled with damp but it was my first place on my own and I loved it.

I elected myself head of the kitchen and rustled up dinner for the three of us most nights. I had a passion for lamb chops, so my mother gave us supplies to take back to Dublin with us. I would stand in the tiny kitchen in that freezing flat making lamb chop dinners with mushy peas and mashed potatoes. My obsession with food had started. The three of us got on great, but not surprisingly, the relationship with my girlfriend didn't last too long. We broke up just before Christmas. She was studying drama in Trinity College and very much into the drama society, which wasn't my scene at all. We grew apart very quickly and the relationship fizzled out. It was a very innocent relationship and we were more friends than anything else; the break up was mutual and we were happy to continue sharing the flat.

Living in Dublin was great because I was out every night. I had freedom for the first time and college was very social. I was on the social committee and was heavily involved in organising the college ball and student union events. I knew everybody and everybody knew me. I was the flamboyant, outgoing one in the group and people definitely knew when I was there. To be fair, I was hard to miss in a full-length herringbone overcoat, red patent shoes and an Al Capone hat. I looked a sight but I thought I was fabulous. I was a student; I didn't give a damn, not a care in the world.

The best part-time job in Dublin at the time was in the Banqueting Hall in the Burlington Hotel, so of course I had to get a job there. It paid five pounds an hour, which was a lot of money at the time. My friend Michael Brennan's father was general manager of the PP Doyle Group and found jobs for us. I worked on Wednesday and Thursday nights until 4 AM. Things were good; I had money in my pocket and I had struck up a friendship with the most beautiful creature I had ever seen. Her name was Naomi O'Connor and she was in my class at college. I had admired her from afar – she was gorgeous, sophisticated and elegant and I felt drawn to her. When I eventually starting going out with her, I felt like the luckiest man in Dublin; she was charming, funny and beautiful. Between working, socialising and Naomi there was very little time for study. I was lucky because the practical subjects came natural to me and I did just enough study to get through subjects like psychology and science. I managed to pass my end of year exams, which was a miracle in itself, but my French lecturer told me I would fail the subject drastically in third year if I did not do something to improve. So Naomi and I, along with a couple of our college friends, decided to spend the summer in Paris.

Some of the group had jobs arranged before we travelled, but I arrived in Paris with no work and very little French. Naomi got herself a position in Myrtle Allen's restaurant, La Ferme Irlandaise, while I traipsed the streets of Paris looking for a job with my CV in English in my hand. Aiming high, I called to all the five-star hotels with my pidgin French looking for a job. It was a disaster and I had no success. But at least I had somewhere to live. There were ten of us staying in one apartment above La Ferme Irlandaise, near Gare du Nord, Rue Saint Denis. It was in the red light district and I knew all the girls, they were great characters. There were four beds in the dining room of the apartment and four more beds in the sitting room. Naomi and I were the privileged ones that got one of the tiny bedrooms because we were a couple. I don't know how I managed it, but I got a job in a tiny boutique hotel behind the Arc de Triomphe, between Avenue de la Grand-Armée and Avenue Foch. Sadly, it is no longer there but it was a beautiful little hotel called La Residence Du Bois – the Resident of the Wood. It was run by a formidable woman – a tyrant, yet gorgeous. She spoke fluent English along with French and sometimes she didn't sleep at all, working twenty-four hours a day. She was an amazing woman. She taught me

French and I was forced to learn quickly as the rest of the hotel staff had no English. As I was made beds in the hotel, the women would teach me French vocabulary – what a sheet was, what a pillowcase was. We started with very basic stuff.

I quickly fell into the French way of life, especially their eating rituals, and I loved it. It was as if a door had opened to a world that I had never known existed. A lot of the guests staying at the hotel were American, which was great because I could speak to them and tell them about the city and where to go. I made a lot of money in tips. I worked from 7 AM until 5 PM and I did everything: I carried luggage, did room service, changed the beds and cleaned the bathrooms. In the evenings I had a job washing pots and pans in La Ferme Irlandaise. The chef was Michael Wrath, who I am still in touch with today. There was a little Irish community; it felt like a home from home. After work, we would head off to the nightclubs. We were wild that summer and often stayed out drinking until 4 AM, to be back in work at 8 AM. Sometimes we got no sleep at all; we were too busy running around that amazing city. I adored hanging out around the Sacré-Coeur and Montmartre, drinking in all the little Irish bars and going to quaint French bistros. We were earning good money but spending a lot too; I loved the shopping area and the fashion in Paris and the little money I had left after partying I spent on clothes. My French was practically fluent after a month; I shaved my head, lost weight and dressed in fabulous clothes. I fell in love with Paris and didn't want to leave.

Despite being in the most romantic city in the world, there was no real romance between myself and Naomi – of course there wasn't – I was gay. She knew I was not interested intimately and it was never going to work. She developed a major crush on a French man, and so did I. He was tall, talented, effortlessly cool in that way French men are, and had a great body. He was also straight. Naomi and I knew the relationship was over but we stayed friends.

When I returned to Ireland I got my own little bedsit on the South Circular Road. I really enjoyed not sharing with anyone and having a place that was all mine. The focus of third year at college was on getting a three-month work placement, doing a thesis and a lot more studying, which was the one thing I didn't enjoy about college. The title of my thesis was 'The Relevance of Disco Bars to the Irish Hotel and Catering Industry'. I was more than willing to throw myself into the topic. There was a lot of research done – I went to every disco bar I could find – always for the benefit of my thesis, of course. The big ones at the time were Rainbows on Exchequer Street and Magnums in the Gresham Hotel.

Despite the pressures of my final year in college, I continued to work one night a week in the Burlington Hotel and three nights in Naas. I developed a strong work ethic at that time and it has stayed with me throughout my career. I also had a real love of partying that stayed with me most of my life too. I became an expert at being able to juggle college, work and partying. I worked in the restaurant in Naas on Sunday and went out afterwards to Nijinksy's nightclub in the Curragh. On Saturday night I never made it out, as it was always too late when I finished work. I hung out with guys I worked with, driving around in cars we were far too young to have. At college I was still involved with all the social clubs and was busy running around organising events and getting myself into trouble.

My class was like a family, we were extremely close. We were all working in hotels and the college was small so there was a close-knit family feel that I loved. I worked Christmas Eve that year and had drinks when I was finished so I missed Christmas Day with my family as I was so wrecked and hungover.

It was a strained Christmas at home to say the least. I used work, college, my friends and partying as escapism, a way of distancing myself from my family. I often felt as though I was searching for my own identity and at times felt claustrophobic. I really think I wanted to rebel against life but was unable to do so. Out of respect for my parents and family I couldn't be an embarrassment. In hindsight, the distance I put between myself and my family was an indication of the confusion I felt about the past and my sexuality. It was like I began running from myself.

I didn't really give a damn about my final exams. It was not until after Christmas that I knuckled down and studied. Just as I had done for the Leaving Cert, I went to the library in Earlesfort Terrace to study. I didn't like sitting in a library with a pile of books, it definitely was not me, but I had to do it and the UCD library had fewer distractions. I had around fourteen subjects to work on, including things like accountancy, economics and sociology. I had to get through them in order to get to do what I wanted to do, and there was no way I was going to repeat the year. Aside from the study, third year was all about getting a work placement; to get your qualification you had to do a three-month stint. A lot of the focus was on getting the placement you wanted – all we talked about was where to go, whether to go abroad or stay at home. I was one of the last, if not the last person in my class to organise a work placement position. I was too busy running around like a nut case, enjoying myself. But somehow I managed to get a work placement, pass my final exams and obtain a B in my thesis.

I secured a six-month work placement with the Royal Marine Hotel in Dun Laoghaire. I was a night manager and it was horrendous. In the kitchen the bottom job is kitchen porter, in management one of the lower-status jobs is night manager. Everybody hates it, for obvious reasons. When my friends were going out I was putting on my suit for work. My role involved a lot of accountancy as I had to do the night audit. It was not boring though and I was kept busy. The audits took about four hours, which was half the night shift gone. We had three ballrooms and seven meeting rooms and they all had to be made ready on my watch. On the weekends when there was a wedding, or three, it would be after 3 AM by the time I managed to throw everybody out, and then I had to cash up the bars and clear up. It was tough work. There were also the security checks, floor walks, as well as a dodgy boiler to contend with. Often I found myself hammering the boiler with a wrench in the early hours of the morning, with little or no idea what I was doing. It was not uncommon for the maintenance guy to get a phone call from me at 5 AM begging for his help, as I explained there would be a lot of irate customers without hot water in the morning.

As the building was so old, there was constantly things going wrong or breaking down. There was never a dull moment at the Royal Marine and I was always on my toes, wondering what the hell was going to happen next. One day a hot water pipe burst in a guest bedroom. I jumped in with a towel to try and contain the water spurting everywhere. I didn't think for a minute about the fact that the water was boiling, even though the steam was quickly turning the bedroom into a sauna. My feet were badly burnt on that occasion, but I just got on with my job. It was all in the line of duty.

My first night as night manager after my training period is etched into my memory for all the wrong reasons. Sitting behind the reception desk on my own at about 4 AM, having just finished the night audit, I saw a customer's car whizzing out of the hotel car park. Surprised, I looked out and saw another car racing off into the distance. It was my first night, I was trusted to do the job on my own and cars were being stolen. Panicking, I stood on the desk desperately trying to catch the number plates of the cars that were being stolen, while dialling 999 to report it to the Gardaí. Two cars were robbed that night and I had the daunting task of telling the guests next morning that their cars had been stolen on my watch, and that the Gardaí were waiting to speak to them. I thought, 'If this is an indication of my career I am fucked!' From that night on I made it my business to get to know the cops. All the Gardaí from the local station came to the Royal Marine after their shifts and I always gave them a couple of late drinks. Car robberies were rife in Dublin at the time, so I happily fed them beer and sandwiches to ensure they would help me out when I needed them.

I had a bedroom in the old part of the building and soon the hotel became my home. It was a novelty at first, but that wore off rapidly. Really it was just an existence, not a life. I worked all night and slept all day. I went to bed at 10 AM via the accounts office, got up at 5 PM, went down to the hotel kitchen and cooked myself something to eat or asked the chef to cook me something. I didn't eat hot food that often, I lived on sandwiches really. During the winter I could end up not leaving the hotel for long periods of time, so I did start going a bit mad. Working and living in the same place is not conducive to a healthy state of mind! On my days off I went home or visited my sister Mary, who was now in college in Maynooth. We went out and got drunk for two days solid and then I went back to my life in the hotel again. It wasn't good. Personally I was a disaster. I didn't do any exercise, I didn't do any social activity – all I did was work and drink.

After working in the hotel for a couple of months a gang of us from college went on a two-week holiday to Marbella to celebrate our exam results. We stayed in a beautiful apartment in the old part of the town, which was owned by one of my friend's parents. I can't believe they trusted a group of seven students to stay in their place, but they did. We had a superb time; I think there were at least sixteen bottles of gin consumed and at that age, a great time meant being drunk for all of it. While in Marbella I met a guy who ran a bar and was the campest person I had ever met. He was outrageous; he had this fabulous bar and knew everybody, and equally everybody knew and adored him. I could see myself in him so much, but was not ready to face up to what that meant. Despite being impressed by this man and really relating to him, I came home and ended up in a relationship with a woman.

I was not back at work after my holiday very long when I met a lady who fell in love with me. She was a receptionist in the hotel. One night, while I was carrying out my night manager duties, she came back to the hotel after she had finished work and had been out for drinks. She expressed her feelings for me and very soon after we became a couple. I didn't think anybody would ever like me like that; I had no confidence in that sphere of my life. I was destroyed, so for someone to come along and tell me straight out that they wanted me was a real shock. And so began my first serious relationship with a woman. She was beautiful, with sparkling green eyes and strawberry blonde hair. I was torn; I really liked her and thought she was lovely, a very attractive lady, a lovely soul, with a beautiful heart and very kind – but sexually there was nothing going on for me. It just wasn't happening. I did sleep with her, well I tried to, but I didn't particularly enjoy it. I did it for her. We did have fun times together. We were proper boyfriend and girlfriend; we arrived everywhere together, went for drinks with friends and to parties. We were like any couple having a good time, except I knew it didn't feel right for me. She met my family and I met hers. My parents adored her and her family loved me. Both mothers were eyeing up hats for our wedding. We moved into an apartment together and appeared to be the perfect couple. I had decided to stop living in the hotel and got an apartment across the road with some colleagues. It was busy the whole time; if I was not working I was partying. A flatmate moved out so my girlfriend moved in and we set up home together. It was considered the natural progression in our relationship and though it did not feel natural to me, I went along with it.

It took me a long time to get a promotion in the hotel as there were simply no positions available. I eventually got a job as day duty manager and threw myself into my new role. The general manager, Pat McCann, who is still in the business, was a very good mentor. I was only twenty-one and I had a job with a lot of responsibility. I happily stepped up to the challenge and did it well. I was able to co-ordinate five weddings on a Saturday afternoon, handle problems and complaints, co-ordinate staff to run bars and restaurants – essentially run the hotel. It was a busy job. On Friday evenings when the boat came in from England we were always overbooked for rooms. I would have to do about ten book-outs, which meant I had to send people who had booked with us to another hotel, and had to pay for them. I use to get shouted at in the middle of the foyer, but I soon learnt how to calm down irate customers.

There was never a dull moment in that hotel. One night, somebody died and I had to get the coroner's office to remove the dead man. A lot of old people frequently stayed in the hotel so there was always someone losing their false teeth. I spent a substantial amount of my time searching hotel rooms for gummy old dears. It was not uncommon either for guests to get locked out of their bedrooms naked. The Irish rugby team stayed one night and there was mayhem as girls ran around the place like rabbits in heat . . . mind you I was not too far behind them myself! When work got too stressful and I was having a bad day, my only saviour was a swift drink. On those occasions I ran through the kitchen, out the back door and across the road where there was a pub. If your head was wrecked and you needed a quick pint, that was the spot. Once I had calmed down and taken a little break I returned to work all smiles, ready to face the guests once more.

The hotel closed on Christmas Eve until St Stephen's Day. Two members of management had to stay in the hotel for security, so myself and another manager agreed to do it. We waved the rest of the employees off as they left to spend the festive season with their families. The hotel was eerily empty with no customers, waiters, receptionists, chefs, or bar people. We decided to make the most of it, so I invited Mary and some of her friends to come and stay in the hotel with us. It turned into a bit of a party. We were like Macaulay Culkin in the movie *Home Alone*; it was a novelty to do the things we would normally not get away with. We picked the most luxurious suites in the place and took them over for the two nights. The kitchen was full of tasty food and we helped ourselves to drinks from the bar. We were running around the place like children in a sweet shop. On Christmas Day, we cooked steak for our dinner. Cooking in a hotel kitchen is very different to cooking at home; everything is on an industrial scale, so we were all running around this massive kitchen trying to find olive oil and butter and other ingredients. We set one of the tables in the restaurant and sat down to our meal and a couple bottles of wine, before retiring to our suites. We lived it up in style that Christmas.

After working in the Royal Marine Hotel for two and a half years I felt it was time to move on. In my experience, two years is about the limit for any hotel job. I had fond memories in Dun Laoghaire and didn't want to ruin them by burning out and becoming bitter or jaded. There were stories filtering back from London of friends working in fabulous five-star hotels. They had these supposedly glamorous lifestyles and I became increasingly eager to try something new. I think my girlfriend knew what was going on. I told her I was going to London for work, even though I was leaving a good job and had nothing set up in London. I just needed to go, it was time. There were at least three 'bon voyage' parties, each lasting several days. It was the long goodbye with us all as drunk as monkeys.

My girlfriend was a wonderful woman but in the end I just couldn't do it any more. I knew she was getting serious about me and was thinking about marriage, but I panicked. I didn't want the wedding or the commitment but I didn't know what to do about it. I didn't know how to handle the conflicting emotions any more. The only escape for me was to run. I was petrified inside so I got on a plane to London. It was the closest I ever came to marriage and my girlfriend was very upset and I felt guilty hurting her, but I couldn't stay and continue to live a lie. We didn't really break up, I just left.

3

London

If a man is to live, he must be all alive, body, soul, mind, heart, spirit.

– Thomas Merton

I was filled with mixed emotions as I sat on my flight to London. I was nervous and full of excitement about what the future had in store for me, but a part of me was wondering what the hell I was doing. My friend Geraldine had a job in a hotel in London and on one of her visits back home she impressed me with stories about a buzzing city of lights, stars and streets paved with gold. Everyone in the industry was talking about the amazing pay and great working conditions in the glamorous five-star hotels in London and for many emigration seemed the best option at the time. There was a massive brain drain from Ireland in the 1980s as young people flocked in their droves to England and America in search of work. My situation was different – I had a permanent steady job, a relationship with a beautiful woman hoping for an engagement proposal, and a great circle of friends. To the outside world I had the perfect life, but I knew I wanted more. The next promotion open to me in the Royal Marine Hotel was the position of general manager. I was twenty-one years old and too young for the job, I felt I needed to learn more. I was career driven and didn't want to get stuck. I was determined to be the best in the game, but as I touched down in the UK, I had my dreams and very little else. I had no job and nowhere permanent to stay.

Geraldine insisted that I stay on her couch until I found my feet. She picked me up from St Pancras train station, where I stood waiting for her with two modest suitcases filled with all my possessions. I was very naïve and as green as you could get. She was renting a room in a small house and I was excited about catching up, setting up base and finding work. However, when we arrived I was not greeted by the welcoming party I had been hoping for; in fact it was quite the opposite. There was a very strange, tense atmosphere almost immediately and Geraldine's housemate looked confused when she saw a guy she'd never met standing in the middle of her sitting room with two suitcases. She asked to speak to Geraldine privately in another room and it quickly became apparent that she was not one bit happy with my plan to occupy her couch. Geraldine had never mentioned to her that I was coming to stay. This woman owned the house and flipped the lid that she had not been filled in about the extra lodger. The next thing I knew I was standing on the street, my life in two bags, in a sprawling city I didn't know. I was only in London an hour and I was homeless – it was a complete disaster. London was already turning out not to be the city I had been dreaming of.

On a piece of crumpled paper stuffed in my pocket, I had a relatively short list of phone numbers of people I went to college with and worked with in Dublin who had moved to London. I traipsed to the nearest newsagent I could find to get change, found a pay phone and started working my way through the numbers in the hope that someone could put a roof over my head for the night. I rang a college friend, Mary O'Leary. In floods of tears on the phone, I told her I had arrived in London with nowhere to stay. Thankfully she took pity on me and I stayed on her couch in her flat in Shepherd's Bush that night.

If a friend was able to offer me a couch to stay on I was so grateful, but I never wanted to outstay my welcome. I was aware they were all sharing with other people and I didn't want to make the situation awkward for them. I always insisted that I had somewhere else to stay lined up and headed off with my two suitcases after a couple of days to repeat the process of ringing the few people I knew in the city. People wanted to help, but often they just couldn't.

I spent a lot of time in an Irish pub called the Bunch of Grapes on the Old Brompton Road, down past Harrods. It became my home from home. A lot of the Irish drank there so I popped in most evenings in the hope of finding a kind-hearted soul who would offer me a sofa or a floor to sleep on that night. If the person I arranged to meet for a pint, with the intention of getting them to offer me somewhere to stay, did not show up or I missed them, then I would simply stay in the pub until some random person offered me a bed for the night. I spent hours sitting in that pub with my two suitcases, slowly nursing a pint and initiating conversations with strangers who might be able to house me for a short time. More often than not my plan worked out; there was real comradeship between the Irish living in London and people were very eager to help each other as much as they could. One night, I got chatting to a bunch of girls from Ireland and as the beer flowed, I told them that my friend, who I was meant to stay with that night, had not turned up. It was a story I told regularly to people I met in the pub. They immediately said I could stay with them. The three women shared a house out by Heathrow and I stayed with them for almost a week. They were very nice and kind, and just wanted to look out for a fellow Irish person struggling to cope in London.

On the nights that I couldn't find someone willing to let me stay on their couch, I had no choice but to book a room in a cheap hotel. I had limited funds with me and hated spending the little money I did have on a disgusting, dingy hotel room. I was constantly afraid that if I ran out of money before I found a job I would be forced to go home. I didn't want to fail or admit to my family and friends that I just could not manage on my own in London. That was not an option for me.

Living out of two suitcases, getting very little sleep and growing more dishevelled by the day, I spent my time trekking from hotel to hotel with my CV, desperate to get a job. But as tired and downtrodden as I was, and often with my suitcases in tow, I was not making a great impression on potential employers. Managers must have been bemused by the sight of a worn-out, bedraggled Irishman, looking like death warmed up, with suitcases in both hands pleading for a job. Looking back, I don't know how I survived those first weeks.

Someone finally took pity on me after a fortnight of relentless job hunting and offered me a position. It was in a gentleman's club in Pall Mall, on the bottom of St James's Street, near St James's Park – and I hated it. The reception I got from customers was less than hospitable because I was Irish. I spent my days listening to members of the club condescend to me in their posh, plummy accents, declaring smugly that I was 'from the wrong side of the fence'. We all worked split shifts so on my break, my mission was always to find somewhere to stay that night. The minute I clocked off I headed straight to the Bunch of Grapes in search of a kind-hearted stranger. Sometimes, if my routine of being stood up by a friend had not worked in the afternoon, I returned to the pub when I finished work that night, if it was not too late, to try again. I stayed working in the gentleman's club for a about a month, but the pay was horrendous, I just couldn't live on it – even without paying rent – so I quit.

I felt so defeated by my first few months in London that I nearly gave up and went home. After weeks of failed job searches and homelessness, I had reached breaking point. One such fruitless day of door slamming and dead ends, I found myself at Heathrow Airport with the intention of getting the first available flight out of London. Exhausted and deflated, all I wanted was the security of my family and friends around me. The knowledge that I had a warm, comfortable bed and a fridge full of food in my parents' house was very appealing. I felt like I just couldn't go on and was prepared to face the humiliation of failure on my return to Ireland. I knew I would feel like a fool going home after struggling to make a success of myself in London but I just didn't care any more.

Lonely and dejected, I fell asleep in the airport. I woke in the middle of the night and sat watching the cleaners, wondering what my next move should be. As dawn broke and London became bright again, I got this renewed determination and decided to give it one more go at making it work. I picked up my two suitcases and headed back to the city in the hope of finally getting a break. I had no job again; I was still homeless with no money for a deposit or a month's rent in advance.I lost about a stone from stress and worry.

After weeks of being turned away from hotel after hotel, I was finally granted an interview for the position of commis waiter in the Rib Room Restaurant of the Carlton Tower Hotel in Knightsbridge. When I walked in the front door of the place I had to fight the urge to turn on my heels and run; I had never seen such grandeur in my life. From the sparkling chandeliers to the plush, inch-deep carpet. I was in awe. As I stood nervously flattening the creases from my now quite shabby suit, I felt completely out of my depth. I sat apprehensively with the food and beverage director, Gerard Sintes. He must have sensed I was overwhelmed by the prospect of working in such a high-end place, but he was a beautiful man who was very kind and put me at my ease. He saw something in me that he liked and gave be the job, much to my disbelief. I had gone from duty manager to commis waiter, but I was prepared to learn everything again. I didn't even know what a cappuccino was; never mind how to make one. We didn't have cappuccinos in the 1980s in Ireland – we had tea and coffee, and a chocolate biscuit if you were lucky. I really had to start at the beginning.

The hotel was very stylish and the dining room was both elegant and formal. On the restaurant floor there was a hierarchy based on experience and length of service, and I was at the very bottom. I was mesmerised by the waiters and their flawless performance on the restaurant floor. They moved effortlessly around the dining room, charming clients and chatting with ease. They were more sophisticated than anyone I had met before and I was completely intimidated by them. I was terrified I would not be able to do what they were doing. For my first month in the job I was not allowed near a table, which was perfectly fine with me as I was scared that I would make a mess of it. I spent hours watching the maître d' and the waiters; the way they served tables and opened wine. I was absorbing and learning new things daily. Step by step, they trained me and my confidence began to grow. The first day I was allowed near a table I was shaking in my boots. All I had to do was serve bread. My aim was to remember the names of the breads and not to let a bread roll fall on the floor, which I managed without too much trouble. The training period was exhausting as I was constantly full of nervous energy.

By this time I had also managed to find a place to live. A woman I worked with in the Royal Marine Hotel was offered a job at the reception desk in the Form Hotel in South Kensington, so she was relocating to London. We decided to get a place together and rented an apartment, sharing with a couple, in Wimbledon. It was definitely an improvement on being homeless, but it was far from perfect. It was quite a nice apartment. However, we had to share a small room with two single beds squashed into it, and the couple we were sharing the apartment with had a newborn baby. Not exactly ideal living arrangements for two people in their early twenties who had expected a partying lifestyle in London, but it was the only thing we could afford until we got on our feet. After a long day working a split shift and commuting forty-five minutes to and from work, I usually just fell into bed. But every night, just as I was drifting off to sleep, the baby would start crying; this went on every three hours, every night, for months. There were prams, baby bottles and nappies all over the apartment, leaving very little room for anything else. The mother of the child wanted the apartment to be spotless to ensure there were no germs that could harm her baby and it bordered on obsessive at times. She was a bit batty and not very friendly. Between the crying baby and his eccentric mother, I wanted to spend as little time as possible in the apartment. I never cooked or ate there, nor did I feel comfortable enough to relax, watch TV or invite friends over. The only thing I did in the apartment, apart from sleep and wash, was my share of the cleaning.

The Carlton Tower Hotel attracted intriguing, flamboyant, charismatic characters of many different nationalities – and that was just the staff, never mind the customers. The hotel was run by a company called Hyatt and employed a mixture of French, English, Australian and Italian waiters, who were a colourful bunch of people. Half of them were gay and half of them were straight. The gay waiters were very camp and unashamedly open about their sexuality, which was a very new experience for me. I gravitated towards the Australian guys because they were the friendliest and the easiest to talk to, and it just happened that most of them were gay. There was Nigel Miller, who everyone knew as Millie. He was around 6'3" and a very handsome, distinguished looking man with huge hands and an even bigger personality. He was flamboyant and quite feminine. David – known as Miss Devlin – was queen bee. An ex-dancer in a drag show in Melbourne, he described himself as a male dancer, who happened to be dressed in women's clothes, and not a female impersonator. He had a very high opinion of himself and aspired to have a lot of money and acquire the finer things in life. He was well-groomed and could be very condescending, but he was great fun. There was his partner, Ian, and there was also Gary Kung, who was one of David's friends from the dance show in Melbourne. On his travels through Europe from Australia, Gary landed in London and got a job in the Rib Room.

David, Gary, Nigel and I worked very closely together in the Rib Room. They taught me so much and I worked hard and learnt very quickly. The clientele were beautiful, elegant and very wealthy. The majority of them came from wealthy old-world families, were extremely gracious and appreciative of the service we provided for them. Camilla Parker Bowles and Sarah Ferguson, before she married Prince Andrew, regularly dined in the Rib Room, as did Sean Connery, Roger Moore, Faye Dunaway, Barbara Windsor and Terry Venables. Frank, a very wealthy Irish businessman who owned a computer business, ate lunch in the restaurant every day and always started his meal with a Bloody Mary. One day I asked him what he would like to eat, as he never read a menu. He said he would love fried chicken and chips from Kentucky Fried Chicken. So off I went out the back door of the hotel, ran down Sloane Street, passed Harrods, in my black uniform and white apron, and into the fast-food takeaway and ordered a Kentucky Fried Chicken snack box. I came back in the door of the kitchen sweating with the order in my hand and all the chefs cooking fine cuisine regarding me with disdain. I put the box full of fried chicken on a plate and wrapped a napkin around the box so no one would spot what I was doing. I arrived at Frank's table and put the food down in front of him. When he realised what it was he laughed his head off. He thoroughly enjoyed his lunch and left me a very, very generous tip. It was completely against the rules to bring food into the restaurant, but what Frank wanted, Frank got.

Frank owned a customised white Bentley, complete with driver. One day during the summer, as he ate his lunch, I was frantically trying to get the lunch service finished and the restaurant closed as soon as I could. He asked me why I was running around manically and I explained to him that my mother and her sister had come over to London to visit me, and if I didn't leave in twenty minutes, I was going to be late collecting them from the train station. Frank just smiled and told me I could take his Bentley to pick them up. My mother and aunt couldn't believe their eyes when I pulled up in the back of a white chauffeur-driven Bentley. They stood frozen to the spot before jumping into the car. They felt like they were in a movie and giggled like two teenagers on the journey to the three-bedroom, ground-floor garden apartment in the middle of Clapton Common, which I had moved into after earning good money for a couple of months. After the driver dropped us off he went back to the Carlton Hotel to collect Frank.

There was never a dull moment in the Rib Room, as many of the clientele were slightly eccentric or quirky. One woman, Mrs Pidgley-Holmes, who came from a wealthy family of developers and builders, always brought her own salad dressing with her. She ordered a salad without dressing and when the food appeared, out came the bottle of low-fat dressing from her handbag. Everything she put into her mouth had to be low fat and she even had her own menu in the place. There was also the 'Ascot Crowd' that frequently stayed in the hotel. The Irish horse trainers always came to the hotel when they were in London. The clientele going to Ascot sipped champagne at 11 AM dressed in beautiful designer clothes. A lot of the customers knew Naas and my mother's children's clothes shop Nippers. All I had to do was mention Nippers in Naas and they knew my mum, and told me all the local news from the area, which made me feel closer to home.

During our breaks between split shifts, David, Gary, Nigel and I headed to the King's Road for something to eat, and very often, a couple of drinks. We would spend a couple of hours in a beer garden, a restaurant or sitting in the park. They were overtly gay and had fabulous stories about their travels across the world, the partners they had had and the shows they had performed in. I was intrigued by their lifestyle and loved how open they were about it. Listening intently as they spoke about ex-boyfriends and relationships, I increasingly found myself identifying with them and felt very comfortable in their company. Encouraged by their frankness, I slowly started sharing some of my secrets too.

The first time I ever said out loud that I was gay, I was with David, Nigel, Gary and a couple of other lads in Henry J. Beans on the King's Road having chicken wings and beer outside in the sunshine. After months of hanging around with them and revealing little bits about myself, they asked me directly if I was gay and I said I was. I waited for their reaction, thinking they might have been slightly shocked, when one of them quipped 'Please, it's written on the wall.' The weight that was lifted off my shoulders that day was immense. I hadn't even realised the pressure I was under until it was gone. Over the coming months they gave me the space to discover things on my own. I was very lucky to have three men protecting me as I came out. They answered all my questions and supported me through the process. They knew I was very vulnerable and that I had been hurt, so they looked after me. I was taught by some very nice people with high morals about homosexuality and gay life. With their help, I found myself and my own identity. My life started on Sloane Street.

Coming out as a gay man in London was an adventure and I did it with great enthusiasm and flamboyance. Everything had to be gay – gay restaurants, gay pubs, and gay nightclubs. I didn't go anywhere if it wasn't gay. There was no straight in my life. I completely submersed myself in this new world, and I loved it. I adored the music, the freedom, the fashion and the outrageous people I met.

However, although I had started having sex with men, I found that I didn't like sleeping with people I didn't know. I almost always had to be drunk to get into bed with somebody. Sex was very weird for me, which I put down to the abuse I experienced as a child. And even though I didn't enjoy having sex with people I didn't know, it almost always had to be anonymous. I was not very good at having a boyfriend and being in relationships. I was completely dysfunctional in that department. I was looking for a relationship – that remains the one thing in my life I have always wanted but never found – and I did make some attempts at having boyfriends, but always ended up with these self-obsessed, self-absorbed assholes. I think subconsciously I always picked the wrong person on purpose, as a way of protecting myself and keeping people at a distance.

But I still enjoyed myself and had a great time meeting new people. Life was good. I lost a huge amount of weight, I was surrounded by great friends and I loved my job. I was working very hard and starting to get very good at it. In time I was promoted to head waiter and began earning a lot of money. I was up and running at twenty-three and everything was going swimmingly.

My sister Mary, along with her boyfriend and some of her friends from our home town, came to visit me not long after I came out of the closet. I decided it was the right time to tell her I was gay, as I wanted to do it face-to-face. We were walking arm-in-arm home from the pub one evening, having a chat and a giggle and almost without thinking, I blurted it out.

Initially Mary was very upset and very angry. When we got back to my apartment she locked herself in my bedroom and refused to come out or talk to me. She was hysterical and crying; at that stage I was frightened. The only thing I could think to do was ring my mother and tell her what had happened. I told my poor mother I was gay over the phone. She wanted to know if I was sure – I told her she had always known. I put Mary on the phone to her and she calmed my sister down. The next day, I told my boss I needed to go home as I had just come out to my mother over the phone. He was an absolutely fabulous man from East London who had worked all over the world. Once he got over the disbelief that I had broken the news over the phone, he told me to take some time off and come back when I was ready.

I went home to speak to my parents. My plan was to deal with it up front, to clear the air. We didn't deal with it, but we tried. My parents were very shocked. They didn't know how to take the news. We sat around the table and I tried to explain to them how I felt, but they really struggled to understand. There were not a lot of people living an openly gay lifestyle in Ireland at the time and my parents most definitely didn't know anyone who was gay, yet here was their son telling them he was homosexual. It was very difficult for them and they really struggled to get their heads around it. But to their credit, they tried to understand and support me, and they slowly came around to accepting it as best they could. Mary came around very quickly too and has proved incredibly supportive ever since.

I went back to my life in London but came home on a regular basis, but more out of duty than anything else. Uncomfortable and self-conscious, I often felt like I had to disguise who I was, lying in some instances, as a lot of people in Ireland still didn't know what my lifestyle in London was like. I was balancing two separate lives for a while and I hated it. I like people to know me for who I am. I would fly back to London after a visit home and go straight from Heathrow Airport to a gay bar in Earls Court, throw my suitcase behind the bar, go onto the dance floor and throw my arms in the air. It was a relief to be around people who were like me, who accepted me. It felt at the time that only my friends truly understood me. I surrounded myself with a tight-knit group of gay people who supported and cared for me.

Meanwhile, back in Dun Laoghaire, there was a poor young lady still waiting for me to propose to her. I came home in June after just coming out and met all my friends in a pub in town – all my old college and work friends. I pulled her over to a corner and told her. I felt terrible and

4

New York

Don't look down on others unless you are helping them up.
– Jesse Jackson

London was my playground and I was having a ball. I had found my feet after living there for eighteen months; I had made the city my home. I loved my job and, with a great circle of friends, I was becoming comfortable in my skin after coming out. But then came an offer that I just could not refuse.

I had applied for a Donnelly visa while at college. I dutifully filled out the application form, sent it off and never thought about it again. That is, until three years later when a letter saying my visa application had been successful was dropped through my letterbox. Donnelly visas were very rare and difficult to get. It was torture trying to decide whether to pack in my job and leave my friends to go to New York. Although the thoughts of leaving the familiar behind were very scary, I knew that my career was going to have to be a major factor in my decision. There would not be any opportunities for promotion for me in the near future. I wanted the position of assistant manager but I knew it would be a couple of years before the person in that role would retire. It was a very difficult decision to make; I was torn between continuing to live in London, where I had established myself after a tough struggle, or take on a new adventure in New York. I feared that if I stayed in London, I would regret passing up the chance to see what New York had to offer and consoled myself with the idea that I could always come back if things didn't work out. I resolved that I would rather regret what I had done than regret what I hadn't, so I quit my job and packed up my belongings. I was heartbroken leaving my friends, but excited about heading to New York. I went home to Ireland first to say goodbye to my family, but once I was resolute about going, I couldn't wait to get on the plane. I left a couple of days after Christmas and was in New York before New Year's Eve.

It was a big move and I only knew one person in New York, my friend Peter, who I had gone to boarding school with and was from Naas. I had nowhere to stay in New York, so my brother-in-law's first cousin, who was a marketing manager for one of the hockey teams in New York, offered to put me up while I got settled. He was a complete jock and I was on the other end of the spectrum. He lived up in Inwood, in north Manhattan, a very old district with a large community of settled Irish people. It was a complete culture shock. It was freezing in Manhattan; I had never felt cold like it before in my life. I had only been staying with him a couple of days when he told me he was going to visit his mother in Connecticut and invited me to go with him. I had just met him and the next thing I knew I was going to meet his family! Not only did I get to meet his mother, we ended up having to stay with her for three days as we got snowed in. Spending three days stuck in a house with two complete strangers was not my idea of fun. And to add to an already stressful situation, I had no change of clothes – a catastrophic style disaster for me. I washed my clothes every evening and dried them on a radiator overnight. When we finally got back to the city, I spent about two weeks sleeping on his couch. He shared his very small one-bedroom apartment with his girlfriend, so not only was I staying with someone I had never met before, I was living in a very small space with a couple. They were very kind to take me in and were a great help, but I couldn't help feeling awkward.

Despite the initial issues with accommodation, I immediately fell in love with New York. Mesmerised by the size of the place and everything in it, I was city-struck; it was like living on a movie set. There was electric energy pulsing through Manhattan. Walking down Broadway, I felt like I was starring in one of the TV shows I had grown up watching. I was in awe, and even though it was freezing cold, it was still buzzing. It was fantastically daunting, but exciting nonetheless.

The first time I ventured around the city on my own was to go to a job interview. I had set up the interview before leaving London, which is the only organised thing I did before flying to New York. The United Nations Plaza Hotel was part of the Hyatt chain, which I had worked for in London. There was no guarantee of a job though, as they were unable to transfer me, so I had to take the risk and come to the US in the hope of getting it. I decided I didn't need to get a cab; that I was well capable of navigating the city on public transport. I jumped on a bus in Midtown and got off on 100th street and Fifth Avenue. As the bus pulled off I noticed the place looked like a ghost town. Surrounded by derelict boarded-up buildings and groups of men hanging around street corners, I knew I was in the wrong place. I had found myself smack bang in the middle of Spanish Harlem, on my own in a smart two-piece suit and overcoat. I might as well have been wearing a T-shirt with the slogan 'Please rob me at knifepoint – I haven't a clue what I am doing'. I tried to keep calm and look like I knew where I was going, but I stuck out like a sore thumb. I walked briskly and purposely for half a block, trying to look causal and as if this is where I had intended to be. A cab driver spotted me before I saw him, drove over to me, rolled down his window and roared 'What the hell are you doing here?' He told me to get into the cab and informed me I was in one of the most dangerous parts of New York, as he sped off at high speed.

As he dropped me off at the United Nations Plaza Hotel on 44th and First Avenue, I thanked him profusely for coming to my rescue. I was more than a little shook up by my experience but I got myself together as best as I could and headed into the interview. I got the job as assistant manager of the Ambassador Grill in the hotel, which was near the United Nations. I thought I was really going places with my new position, until I discovered that assistant managers in New York get paid pittance, just $300 a week. I couldn't live on the wages I was earning, but thankfully I had some money saved from London when I was on a good salary. The position of assistant manager was very different in America to what it is in Ireland and the UK. It was an administrative role – answering the telephone for reservations and devising table plans. I didn't get to know the customers, as managers don't serve tables to avoid encroaching on the waiters' role. I missed buzzing around the restaurant talking to the clients and getting to know the regulars. I started work at 2.30 PM every day, having my breakfast in the hotel in the afternoon, and worked until midnight. Every Sunday, many of the Jewish community from the Lower East Side came in for brunch and were very demanding; they kept everyone on their toes. Cocktail hour was also very busy with people coming in after work and meeting people for dates. But there really wasn't a lot for me to do, in comparison to how busy I had been in the restaurant in London, so I got bored very quickly. That said, with the memory of being homeless and jobless in a big city fresh in my mind, I was grateful to have found work.

Once I had settled into work, aware that I was coming close to the point of overstaying my welcome at my brother-in-law's cousin's home, any free time I had was spent trying to find my own place. However, finding an apartment in Manhattan that I could afford with my pay packet was mission impossible. Everything I looked at was outrageously expensive and way out of my league. Most people in my position end up living in some dump in downtown Manhattan, and sure enough that is where I eventually set up home. I managed to get an illegal sub-let apartment downtown. My childhood friend Peter, who ran a little restaurant in Midtown, knew a woman at work who was leaving her flat to move in with her boyfriend. He told me it was available and I jumped at it. I was sick of sleeping on a couch and living out of my bag. It was a corporation apartment on 4th Street and Second Avenue. I was not in glamorous Manhattan any more; I was with the real world. I didn't even get the opportunity to see the flat before I agreed to take it, so pretty soon I found myself standing in the middle of 4th street, somewhere between Second and Third Avenue in the Lower East Village, with my belongings scattered on the pavement. I had the key for the apartment but had to go find it. It was number six and the apartment was 2B on the top floor, five flights of stairs and no elevator. It was an old building with narrow staircases. The paint was peeling off the walls; it was dilapidated, it was run down, and it was corporation.

I got to the top floor and the door of my new apartment was swinging open – not the best of starts. There had been a fire in the building recently and the apartment had been re-done to a very basic standard. There was lino on the floor, but the walls were freshly painted and there were three sparsely decorated rooms. There was a small living room, even smaller kitchen, and a tiny bedroom. I soon realised that there was no electricity and the few appliances that were in the apartment, weren't working. There was heating though, which was a good thing considering it was -15°C. I got a locksmith in to fix the broken door and I rang the electricity company from a payphone to get the power turned on. By that night I could lock my door and be safe and warm. There was heating, electricity and very little else, but it was my own place.

The next day I walked around the area; it was a very lively place. I was terrified but I took the bull by the horns and found a futon shop and bought one. I had slept on the bare floor on my first night in the flat and I was not planning to do that again. I carried the futon up the five flights of stairs. When I say I sweated going up and down those stairs I mean I sweated. I found a working TV in a second-hand shop, a small kitchen table and chairs, as well as peach and black sheets, which I made into curtains. It was very basic, but after I had furnished the place it was quite cosy.

The street where I lived was also home to drug dealers and users on one side and hookers on the other. The place came alive at night and after midnight it was wild. It was great fun going out on the street, especially when the weather improved, as there were always colourful characters hanging around day and night selling things. The items they were selling were generally stolen from people and properties in the local area. You could go and buy back all your stolen goods on this street, where they were flogged openly, and if your apartment was robbed this was the first place to go looking for your stuff. In London I had worked in Belgrave, darlings, which was all rather posh and populated by the affluent in designer labels – Giorgio Armani, Gucci and Cartier all had shops on that road. I was surrounded by that glamour and it was a lovely place to be. This was very different – I was in lower Manhattan and I had to take off my watch and dress down just to leave the house to go to work. My normal attire leaving my flat was a scruffy T-shirt and shorts, simply because I didn't want to get mugged. When I arrived to work I changed into my suit and could put my Cartier watch back on my wrist. I learnt very fast how to survive in New York.

People say that if you can survive in New York, you can survive anywhere, and I certainly found that to be true. It was pre-Giuliani era and parts of the city were being run by gangs and drug dealers. I realised very quickly that if the people hanging out on the street knew you, nobody else would go near you, so I went out of my way to get to know the locals. There was a guy who owned a shop beside my flat who sat at the door of my building every day. His shop was the dirtiest little place I had ever seen in my life; I never bought anything from him but I always stopped to say hello and have a chat. He was in the same place every day and knew exactly who was on that street and what they were doing, whether they were selling or buying. Once I got to know him and he grew familiar with me, I felt safe. I made sure I knew everybody on the street; I didn't care if they were hookers or drug dealers, I spoke to all of them. After a couple of months I knew all of them and I walked up and down that street at any time of day without a problem. In the summer months it was like a constant party on the street because it was so hot and there was no air conditioning in the buildings, so people sat on the street. My aunt Angela Kelly came to stay with me on a stop-over from New Zealand to Ireland and she was more than a little shocked at my living arrangements. She only stayed one night and voiced her concerns about the area, but once she knew I was happy and felt safe she was fine.

However, as comfortable as I was in my neighbourhood, there were some bleak sides to it. My next-door neighbour, for example, was a crack addict. Crack cocaine was rife in New York at the time and she was a disturbing embodiment of that prevalent sub-culture. The smell of crack every night almost made me physically sick and the hallway was constantly engulfed by a disgusting, chemical stench. I tried to avoid her as much as I could, but one night, while I was chilling out watching TV after work, there was a bang on my door. When I opened up, there standing in front of me was my neighbour. She looked like a skeleton, like death with a pulse. I was face to face with what seemed like half a woman. Her face was sunken and gaunt and she was painfully skinny. It was a horrific sight. I stood frozen to the spot and the hairs stood up on the back of my neck. I had never met someone like her before; she was completely crazy. She was looking for a bowl of sugar. I have never filled a bowl of sugar so quickly; I just wanted this person away from me. It was my first real exposure to drug addiction and that drug culture and it truly shocked me.

I usually explored the city at night. I didn't know many people and really had to establish a social life for myself all over again. I worked from 2.30 PM in the afternoon until midnight and then went out to a few bars on my own, trying to figure out the gay scene and make some friends. I spent a lot of time venturing around Manhattan alone, discovering the city and trying to meet people. As spring approached and the weather started to improve, New York became a much more pleasurable place to be. It was quite easy to go out to bars, clubs and restaurants on my own, and going out to socialise was not that expensive with concessions and cheap drinks. The energy in the city was great and there were so many places to discover and explore. I would pour myself a couple of gin and tonics at home for a bit of Dutch courage and then head out on my own. I got my hands on a gay magazine and worked my way through the list of bars and clubs of different genres, including S&M bars, disco bars, cocktail bars, Uptown bars and Midtown bars. I went to them all. I don't know how I got out alive from some of the places I visited by myself. The Meatpacking District on the West Side Highway was full of S&M bars. I wanted to see everything and know what was available

I had a half bottle of gin in me before I ventured into my first S&M club. Dressed in jeans and a fitted black t-shirt – the standard gay uniform the world over – I headed to an address I'd found in a gay magazine. I arrived at a warehouse with a big steel door. I took a deep breath and knocked. A small hatch on the door slid open, a man said something incoherent to me, the hatch was shut again and the door opened loudly. I was ushered downstairs to what looked like a dungeon in the basement. It was an old, dimly lit stone warehouse; there was a bar in the corner of the room and I made my way over to a background of pumping dance music and the smell of poppers. As I sipped my drink, my eyes adjusted to the dark space and I noticed a labyrinth of dark rooms set off from the bar. In the middle of the floor in the first there was what appeared to be a group of men carrying out a sex act, which involved a sling. In another room, a naked guy was tied with rope to some sort of platform, with candles placed all around him. It was very gothic and looked almost like a torture chamber. I wasn't quite sure what was going on – all I knew was it was not the Welcome Inn on Parnell Street. If it was art or sex I wasn't quite sure, but I wasn't hanging around to find out. The whole thing terrified me. I was open to new experiences and eager to find out what I did and didn't like, but that scene was definitely not for me.

One bar I did love was the Eagle on West Side Highway. It's gone now, but it was a great place in its day, with a more friendly atmosphere than some of the other gay bars I had ventured into. It was made very famous by a couple of movies, so of course I wanted to go and see it. When I first walked in, I was a bit taken aback by the sight of all the men in their skimpy leather outfits. But of course it was nowhere as shocking as the S&M club I had visited. I sat at the bar and had a couple of drinks just taking in everything that was going on around me. Often when I went to a bar or club I would just have a couple of beers, not talk to anyone and then just go home. But eventually I got so comfortable in the Eagle I became a part of the scene there, which I really wanted. When I took people who had come to New York to visit me to the Eagle they were shocked, but for me it had become normal. The clubs in New York were phenomenal including Mars, which had five floors, each with different music and clientele. There was always somewhere to go and something to do.

After a short time, I started to make some friends at work. I became friendly with two cocktail waitresses, Donna and Elaine, who were also, of course, trying to make it in the modelling world. Donna ran a modelling school for kids in Manhattan, along with modelling herself and working in the hotel. Elaine was also involved in commercial modelling, along with her waitressing job. Everyone in New York is either a jobbing actor or model. They were quite weary of me initially, as I wasn't a New Yorker and had a different mentality and energy about me, but eventually they accepted me. We began going out clubbing together and had really fun nights.

I also got to know Richard Atkins, the piano player in the hotel who was also a playwright, a musician and a lovely man. He was married to a woman of Irish descent and he became one of my closest friends in Manhattan. I leaned on him for support quite a lot. Whenever I was feeling homesick, lonely or down I knew that I could talk to Richard.

After he was finished entertaining guests we would sit after work and have a drink and a chat. He was a very good listener. On our days off we enjoyed going for dinner and a couple of drinks together. I absolutely adored him.

Life in New York could be difficult emotionally, and at times I felt very isolated. In order to deal with the parts of me that I kept buried, that I considered damaged and dysfunctional, I began to build up a defence mechanism to hide my vulnerability. I constructed a character, like an alter-ego, to protect myself and I became very loud – New York loud. I discovered that if I talked really loudly, like most other people in the city did, it gave people a clear message not to screw with me. I adopted this personality because in my early experience of New York, people had considered my openness and naïvety a weakness and had pushed me aside. I couldn't let that happen to me; I practically had to fight my way around the city.

On a bus journey one day, I encountered a female driver who, at first glance, reminded me of a big-bosomed mother I would like to hug. But when she opened her gob I realised I wouldn't dare cross her even if someone paid me a million pounds to do it. She was a scary, animated woman with nails like weapons. She was heavily made up, with false eyelashes to boot, and her hair was pulled back severely. Larger than life, she drove the bus with a tyrannical prowess, chewing gum and shouting continuously at her customers. As I stepped up and fumbled around for a ticket, she roared at me 'Honey, get on my bus or get off my bus, make up your goddamn mind!' She shouted at others to 'move it, people' and continued chomping noisily on her gum. She didn't give a shit about anybody. She was so fabulous and scary at the same time that I kind of wanted to be her. I wanted to be that fabulously intimidating. I was so intrigued and in awe of her that I stayed on the bus way past my stop just to watch her. I wanted to be that invincible, so I developed this very brash attitude. I was a bit like a sponge and took on aspects of people's personalities that I admired or envied. I didn't know who I was, and I had no idea what I stood for, so I concentrated my efforts on carefully copying other people. I developed this huge personality that protected and disguised the uncertainty I felt inside. As a result, I was a fantastic party person; a great socialiser who could talk to anyone, could walk into a room and not give a shit. At work my manager persona was part of it. It became an integral part of me. Slowly and carefully, that damaged little boy inside me slipped further from the surface. Soon he had no identity at all. He was sitting in a dark room with the lights off.

This 'new' me soon developed a large circle of friends. The intensity of the city was overwhelming at times; there were just so many people in a relatively small area. The city is unbelievably fast-paced, frantic even, and its inhabitants are equally so, talking fast and loud and everything a drama. One of the women I made friends with at work was, similar to many New Yorkers in my experience, completely neurotic. Going to a restaurant for dinner with her was exhausting as she rambled on with 'I don't eat this, I don't eat that, and how many calories do you think is in that? I will have a salad but hold the dressing'. And that was only ordering the meal. The conversation would go something like this: 'Should I call him? Should I wait for him to call me? Why has he not called me? If I call him what do I say? OK I called him once, should I call him again?' This would go on for the duration of the meal and I would be thinking to myself, My God you people are nuts . . . and they really were. After going for a meal with her I was knackered.

After a while, the craziness of the city, its high-octane energy and its people started to get to me. The heat in Manhattan in the summertime didn't help. I never experienced heat like it. I bought an air conditioner because I couldn't sleep on my little futon in my small room because it was so hot.

I began drinking quite heavily in New York, which wasn't helped by my late-night lifestyle, but I felt at the time that it gave me the courage I needed to venture out around the city and helped maintain the personality I had so carefully constructed. The drinks are stronger in America, so after two Tanqueray gin and tonics I was smashed. One night I was drinking gin and tonic out of plastic glasses at a nightclub downtown and was pretty drunk. I put my drink on the bar and turned around to watch what was happening on the dance floor and when I turned back again, it was gone. I couldn't figure out where it had gone, so I bought another drink, took a sip out of it, put it on the bar, turned around to watch people on the dance floor, turned to get it again and it was gone again. This happened four or five times before, in my haze, I figured out what was going on. The goddamn bar was sloped! it was so dark in the club and I was not quite sober enough to notice that every time I turned around, my drink would simply slide off the bar. I looked down at the floor and all my glasses were lying there in a pool of gin and tonic. The barman was in stitches laughing at me as he had watched the whole comedy sketch unfold.

After a night out I went to the same little diner just around the corner from my flat to get something to eat. I always got the same thing – a toasted turkey club on wholemeal bread with extra mayo and french fries on the side. That was an easy order to say after a good few gin and tonics. After a while the guy in there got to know me and knew what I was looking for so would start making my sandwich the minute I walked in the door. After eating, I slept until it was time for my shift at the hotel to start.

New York is where I took cocaine for the first time. The piano player in the Ambassador Grill, Richard, introduced me to these guys who were two gay actors. They were slightly older and took me out to a bar where we took cocaine. It was an after-hours bar in the Garment District with a big steel door that they banged closed behind you. Inside, it was like an old-style sweet shop with an ice-cream fridge filled with bottles of beer. That was it, there was nothing else, the shelves were bare; it was derelict. Sitting at the end of the bar there was a big guy wearing a big black coat and a Crombie-style hat. He was a drug dealer and, although he couldn't have looked more like a clichéd pantomime dealer, this was quite real. I was given a wrap of cocaine and went into the toilet and took my first line. The immense rush consumed my entire body. I felt amazing; completely invincible, and my confidence levels went through the roof. I went back out into the bar and held court for the whole night. I was the life and soul of the gathering in the pub. And even though it was the dingiest place on earth, it seemed quite fabulous to me. My friends were regular users and they talked me through it. The first line is probably the best line you are ever going to have. After that it is never as good. I felt amazing for about three days. When I woke up the next morning and felt the sensation still in my hands and muscles as I stretched, I felt wonderful. I went back to work the next day. As the cocaine was so pure there was no come down.

On a night out with friends in the Monster Club in Greenwich Village, I spotted this gorgeous, all-American guy in the crowd. We got talking and he was really nice, funny and entertaining, and we hit it off immediately. We swapped phone numbers at the end of the night and the next day he rang me and we arranged to meet for a date. We met for drinks and dinner and talked all night. After that we spent all our spare time together just hanging out in bars, clubs, and restaurants. We enjoyed going for walks in the park and going for coffee together. He lived upstate so he often stayed with me. During sex he was always very safe with me and I sometimes wondered why he was so cautious. But I was falling in love with him and really beginning to enjoy being in a relationship, which I never had before.

After a couple of months together we were sitting outside a restaurant enjoying a meal when he said he had something he needed to tell me. He came right out and announced that he was HIV positive. I was devastated. I broke down in tears. I felt totally betrayed, shocked that he had kept this from me for so long. I had let my barriers down with him and let him in and I was so hurt and let down. I was also terrified. I had never been confronted so closely with AIDS and someone who was HIV positive. The virus exploded in London around 1989, but in the US it had appeared a few years earlier. Treatment at that time was still pretty basic, with combination therapy not yet common practice. It was frightening being a gay man at that time. I freaked out; I couldn't handle the fact that a man I had had sex with, who I was falling in love with was HIV positive. I was very honest with him and told him there and then that our relationship was over. He came back to my flat and we spent the night together but he left the next morning. I met him six months later in a bar and we spent hours sitting in the corner talking. I apologised to him for treating him the way I did, for running when he told me he was HIV positive. He completely understood why I did it and told me he regretted not being honest with me from the start. I never saw him again after that night.

I had a return ticket for Ireland, so in June I went back home for a flying visit to see my family and friends. Before my trip I moved out of my flat and when I got back I moved in with Donna. She had a lovely two-bedroom apartment in Stuyvesant Town on 16th street and Fourth Avenue. It was more residential and quieter than living downtown. More settled and relaxed, living there my life began to take on a level of normality. There was a great little local bar in the neighbourhood called the Dakota. Regulars played pool and darts and I loved meeting my friends there for a couple of drinks. The bar staff knew us all well and if we had one too many, they put us in a cab and sent us home. After work one night I went to meet friends in the Dakota and I instead found myself a gorgeous new boyfriend. I was sober and was introduced by friends to this fabulous 6'2" black guy. He was strikingly handsome and he adored me. I was delighted with myself – a fabulous boyfriend and a nice place to live.

However, a month later the food and beverage director from London came through New York on his way to Manila. Without even thinking, I announced to him that he had to get me out of New York immediately. I did love the freedom of the city, the madness and the anonymity. I could do anything and be anything and nobody gave a shit. I could scream my head off in restaurants and it was completely acceptable; I could drink the head off myself and it was completely acceptable. But despite the appearances of a fun and exciting lifestyle, and although I had never acknowledged it, I knew I had to get out of New York. I knew I was not going to make any money, I knew I was not going to make a career for myself. There was a huge division between independent restaurants and hotels – the business just wasn't the same as it was in London and I was not in the right area for my career. The whole thing was not really working for me; it was not sitting right with me. It was too crazy and I was too manic so I just had to get out. On his return to London, the manager duly let his team know that I was eager to return to the Rib Room.

The restaurant manager rang me in November to tell me there was a job as assistant manager available in the hotel and I jumped at the chance. I ended it with my boyfriend because ultimately I wanted to be back in London alone more than I wanted to be in New York with him. It was a hard decision but I knew I needed to go back to London. I had had enough of Manhattan. I made four times more money in the job I had been doing in London and I was ready to go back to my life there. I was back in London and working in the Rib Room by Christmas.

5

Party Years

Survival is triumph enough.

– Harry Crews

Arriving back in London was like coming home. Most of my close friends were still there and I was delighted to be back in their company. Starting back at the Rib Room was like a homecoming too; I knew most of the staff and they knew me. The only difference this time was that I had swapped the waiter's uniform for a suit. The role of assistant manager came naturally to me. I loved meeting and chatting to the clientele and making sure their needs were met. They all wanted to know about my time in New York and I relished entertaining them with fabulous stories of my adventures in the city that never sleeps. I made the restaurant my own; it became my domain. I was comfortable there and happily waltzed around the floor, charming everyone that came to dine there. The hectic Christmas season was in full swing by the time I returned to London and I certainly hit the ground running at work. There were business people meeting clients for festive drinks, work parties, families reuniting for dinner and frantic shoppers laden down with bags in need of cocktails and a bite to eat. It was busy and I loved it.

In New York I had missed the contact with customers and being able to get to know them. I was now able to be among the customers, chatting, laughing and ensuring they got excellent service. I was in my element. the Rib Room is where I wanted to be. I didn't even have to go flat hunting. I had met a woman called Sameena from London while I was living in New York who had an apartment in Clapham. She had stayed on in America and her apartment was empty so I rented it. I was instantly settled in London with everything falling into place.

I felt more international; more travelled and worldly. I was no longer an Irishman living in London. I had survived New York and now I was back. But if I had brought back a new sophisticated attitude, I had also acquired a terrible accent. I had this garish New York thing going on. I was just so loud and my default response to everything had become 'Oh. My. God.' I had built up this persona to protect myself in America and had come to a point where I didn't even realise I was doing it any more. But I stood out like a sore thumb now that I was back in London. The annoying accent didn't last long as my friends were the first to tell me it was grating on their nerves and to pack it in. I was unceremoniously told by my close mates to drop the Americanisms and I did.

I was back hanging out with Gary, David and Nigel. It was wonderful to be back with these guys, they were so much fun to be around. There was also Scott, who had worked in the Rib Room for a while but lost his job while I was in New York. He worked in a different restaurant in the city but also had a very lucrative secret job on the side. Scott was hyper, clumsy and not very respectful of anything. He was the problem child of the group, always hovering over the self-destruct button. But he was also extremely charismatic, fun and willing to talk. He could be annoying sometimes, but he was always up for a party. Glen Donovan ran a very elite travel agency in London, which is still going today. It is so exclusive it doesn't even have a website, it is by appointment only. Glen liked the finer things in life and knew how to treat himself very well. His partner, Ian, was a merchant banker. There were also a few fashion designers, hairdressers and accountants and together we made a motley crew. We were all well-educated men, with good jobs and high disposable incomes who worked extremely hard but also liked to party.

It was 1991 in London and the gay club scene was buzzing. Of course, our group was well known in the nightclubs because we were young, fabulous and attractive. We were not bitchy or condescending to other people, we just wanted to have fun. I, in particular, was a real party boy. I was always going out and because of my personality I knew a lot of people, and was able to chat away easily. We all loved fashion and were hitting the dance floor dressed head to toe in designer clothes, from John Paul Gaultier to Moschino. We were young enough to be able to go clubbing at night and still go into work and do our jobs well the next day. I worked split shifts, which started at 10 or 11 AM and finished at 3 or 4 PM, depending if I was on the late or early roster. During my few hours off in the afternoon, I normally went to the gym with a couple of guys from work as we were all very conscious about looking good. We were always trying to lose weight and build up chest, arms, legs or butts in order to look fabulous on the dance floor. At around 6 PM we rushed to a restaurant and wolfed down some food, as we would usually only have forty-five minutes before we were due back at work. I worked until 11.30 PM or midnight and then would hit the clubs three or four times a week with my friends. It was very sociable. We did not go out to get drunk; it was all about hanging out together having a couple of cocktails and dancing, and maybe meeting a guy. I was always worried I would miss something if I didn't go out. We went to G-A-Y on a Monday, which was always fabulous, and Heaven on a Wednesday. We would hit the dance floor until 3 AM and then go home to bed to make sure we were all set for work the next day. I didn't go out that often at the weekends as it was too busy at work.

I was never really very promiscuous. I suppose because of my past that just wasn't part of the attraction for me. It was more just a release to go out dancing and see what was happening. I was never really looking for a man when I was out clubbing, it was more about hanging out with my friends and having a laugh. However, one night, when I least expected it, I met a lovely man called Alan Cross. Some of my mates knew him and introduced him. He was a DJ, which was very cool, and had a great personality. He was very funny, outgoing, intelligent and tall. He was a DJ in a lot of big clubs in London and on my nights off I went with him, helping him to carry his vinyls. I stood for most of the night with him at the DJ box drinking cocktails. When I was working I went to the club he was playing in after I finished my shift. We hung out together for a couple of months but it didn't last. I wasn't relationship material, I was too damaged. I didn't know how to handle myself in a relationship so I ended up screwing the whole thing up. I finished it.

Relationships were out for me. I tried but it just didn't work. I became the entertainer in the group instead of looking for sex or a relationship. I was very positive and high energy, so people loved being around me. I kept all the confusion and pain hidden inside most of the time. I became the ultimate party person.

When we first started clubbing it was just cocktails and dancing. But the club scene was moving very fast and it changed rapidly. It was the early 1990s and ecstasy began to hit the dance floors. London became a very exciting place to be. Ecstasy appeared in 1989 and by 1992 it was a fully-fledged part of the scene. It was not like in New York where drugs were underground and people had to go to dingy little pubs to get it. In London it was an integral part of the clubbing experience and everybody was doing it. Dropping an ecstasy pill was just like having a pint for a lot of people. It was everywhere. I went to parties where it was on trays being offered around like canapés. It was almost like a natural progression for me to start taking drugs. It was like I needed to go faster. Alcohol was not enough for me, or maybe it was too much because I got too messy, and booze put too much weight on so I needed something else.

The first time I took ecstasy I was on a dance floor in a club called Heaven with Scott and Gary. I was nervous about taking it but the two boys stayed by my side the whole time. The music was pounding and the rush was out of this world. When I came up on the drug I didn't know what was going on; I had never felt anything like it before. The lads just grabbed my t-shirt and ripped it off me. The energy pulsed through my body and I got lost in the beat of the music and the lights. I loved everyone that night and spent hours dancing my head off.

After that night I took drugs regularly on big nights out but I was always very careful as I didn't like losing control. I knew it was a dangerous thing to mess with. I always knew where I got them from and I always knew how they would affect me before I took them. When you mess around with drugs you have got to look after your friends and they have to look after you. We stuck together; we were not stupid about what we did.

The weekends of doing drugs were planned with military precision and happened around once a month. There was no way we could do it every weekend. Normally it was a Saturday night and there would be something on, like Gay Pride or New Year's Eve, or the Midsummer's Night Ball. On those weekends we planned our outfits, bought our drugs, and got our tickets. We were extremely organised. We loved going to the Fridge in Brixton or Heaven. Trade, a world renowned club for dance music, started at around 4 AM so went there from whatever bar we were in. The DJs at Trade were amazing and a lot of the big names in music started in that club. It was in a basement and it was geared solely towards hardcore music and a lot of drugs. It was a sub-culture that defined the 1990s and we were a part of that. We stayed out all night long or sometimes even the whole weekend. We went out on a Friday night sometimes and wouldn't get home until the Monday morning, if we had enough drugs in our pockets. We went from one club to the other. I sometimes had a pit stop at home to have a shower and a costume change, have a little something to eat, if I could get it down my neck, and then back out again.

We had great nights out together and we travelled as a group. When we went on holidays there was always nine or ten of us. When we went on weekends away there was always a crowd of us, so people gravitated towards us. Glen, being a travel agent, organised all our holidays and they were always fabulous. We did it in style. We stayed in beautiful places in exotic locations and had a ball. We went to cities I had never been to before. It was so exciting. Barcelona was amazing, Amsterdam was fantastic. It was a whirlwind – airports, trains, planes, taxis.

We were always going somewhere, or coming back from somewhere, and it was always a party. In 1994 we went abroad nearly every month. In January we went to Miami, in February we went on another holiday, March was the Queen's birthday so that was another weekend away, April was Barcelona and that summer we went to the opening and closing parties in Ibiza. We flew to New York and did the Black Party, a world-renowned circuit party consisting of about 8,000 queens in leather in the Roseland Ballroom. These circuit parties go all around the world – the White Party in Miami, the Black Party in New York, the opening and closing parties in Ibiza – and we tried to get to as many as we could. They were extravagant, decadent affairs and people spent a lot of money on costumes. I didn't do costumes, as such, but a lot of people did. They were fantasy nights and they were amazing. The sound systems were astonishing, and there were outrageous acts – trapeze artists, fire eaters and drag queens – performing throughout the venue. It was pure decadence and the bigger the clubs, the better the drugs, the more fun we had. The club scene in London was progressing, getting bigger and harder. It was taking a lot more planning to be able to balance work and the clubs because we were doing a lot more drugs. It was not just ecstasy, there was also cocaine. The heady combination of parties and pills proved a catalyst for self-destruction, which truthfully for me, started around this time.

In 1994, a group of ten of us went to the Black Party in New York. There was Gary, Scott, Glen, Ian myself and a few other lads. We flew over to New York and stayed in the Paramount. I had been travelling to New York a couple of times a year to ensure I kept my green card and it felt like a second home by then. I knew the place very well and had friends in the city so I was put in charge of getting everyone their drugs for the weekend. It was a Friday night when we landed and the first thing we did was organise our recreational pharmaceuticals. I rang a guy I knew, who knew a drug dealer, and armed with a spreadsheet of everyone's order, we arranged to meet him that night in Greenwich Village. We headed to a trendy gay restaurant called the University Bar and Grill and sat around a big table for a delicious dinner, washed down with plenty of cocktails. I got a call to say that a limousine would pull up outside and the person with our drugs would be in it. It was around 10.30 PM when I spotted this enormous limo with blacked-out windows drive very slowly past the restaurant and then stop. Ian came out with me and, intimidated and nervous, we got into the back of the limo with a pocket full of money. We were met by two colossal men of pure muscle. They sat either side of a rather less impressive drug dealer, who was a tiny, nondescript-looking guy. He handed me ten envelopes, each with a person's first name, the list of drugs provided and the amount owed. He was the most organised drug dealer I had ever met; I was very impressed. The bill came to $2,000 and as I counted it out, I realised some bitch of a queen had left me $100 short. I frantically counted again, trying desperately to disguise the terror that was setting in. Here we were, locked into a limo with a drug dealer and his heavies and I was $100 short. You could cut the tension in the back of that limo with a knife. I was envisaging my poor parents being told my body had been found in the Hudson. Thank Christ Ian stepped in and handed over the $100 needed. We couldn't get out of that limo quick enough.

Once I got over my ordeal the envelopes were passed out and the fun began. Saturday night was the big party and Manhattan was full of skimpily dressed, leather-clad gay men. The atmosphere was electric. We got dressed in our hotel. I was modestly dressed – in black leather trousers, a t-shirt and a dog collar – but some of our friends were a lot more flamboyant in their attire. One of the guys was sporting chaps, a codpiece, a bare arse and very little else. We walked from the hotel to the Roseland Ballroom, so safe to say he got a few stares from passers-by. On our arrival we realised that there were changing rooms where everyone else was changing into their revealing leather outfits, which would have saved his blushes, as well as his extremities from the cold! The party was phenomenal. It was the first circuit party I had attended and I was enthralled. There were live sex shows, which were quite shocking; my eyes were well and truly opened that night. The music was pumping and the dance floor was thronged with people lost in the music. It was euphoric. We danced until 8 AM, went back to the hotel for a couple of hours' sleep and then got back up and did it all again the next night. I was hooked on the Black Parties from that weekend on.

Amsterdam was another destination we loved to visit. On one trip twenty of us travelled by bus and ferry to celebrate the Queen's birthday there. Twenty queens on a bus for hours with cocktails! It was chaotic to say the least. We were high as kites by the time we got to Amsterdam. One of the lads played air hostess the whole way there, making cocktails for everyone as best he could on a bus. I was drunk and completely out of it by the time we made it to Amsterdam. Gary had to put me to bed when we arrived for a couple of hours to sober me up. Once I woke up I went clubbing. I couldn't eat a thing because I was so sick; I just did more drugs and took more alcohol to keep going. It was two days and nights of solid partying with just a couple of hours' sleep. I was a mess on that break. It was a weekend of debauchery. There was definitely no sightseeing done.

The first time I went to Ibiza was for the opening parties. There were eight of us on that adventure and Glen had booked a villa and two cars for us. We had to be at Gatwick Airport at a ridiculous time, as the flight was at 6 AM. I was working the night before, so after my shift was over I only got an hour's sleep before I had to head to Victoria Station where we were all meeting at 3.30 AM to get the train to Gatwick.

Gary and I had been at work but the rest of the boys came straight from a party. They had taken their suitcases with them to the party and arrived at Victoria Station out of it. We all got on the Gatwick Express and it was all a little bit messy to say the least. Scott, of course, was in full flight, screaming his head off. However, it was not long before we were all in a similar state to Scott. Once we were on the train someone produced a half gram of cocaine and we did a couple of lines on the train to keep us going. Our plan was to stay up all night; no one was going to sleep.

We got to the airport and I gathered up all the passports; I was relatively coherent at that point and there were no way some of them would have gotten on the flight if they had to check themselves in. Glen, Gary and I went to the desk and we checked in as a group. That's when the fun started. The woman asked us, 'Any hand luggage?' and I replied 'Just handbags, darling', 'Did anyone else pack your bag?' and I quipped, 'If she packed my bag darling, God knows what's in it, but probably just bikinis and day wear.' It was a miracle we were all allowed onto that flight. Seriously, who wants to be tortured by a bunch of queens at five o'clock in the morning? We went through customs and duty free and got bottles of vodka, Jack Daniels and gin. We divided up who bought what to ensure there was enough of everything. Plus, of course, we always bought a couple of bottles of champagne. We got seating together on the plane; the party had well and truly started.

When we arrived in Ibiza it was around 8.30 AM. We were met by the sales rep for the villa. She was a posh lady wearing a pearl necklace, a smart dark navy suit, a big pair of sunglasses, red lipstick and sensible shoes. She was looking for the Donovan and Healy party. Glen, who was wearing a tight t-shirt – to show off his arms and pecs – camouflage trousers and a pair of boots, went up to her. The rest of us were sitting around on suitcases half-exhausted from the cocaine on the Gatwick Express and having cocktails on the plane. Some of the boys had been up all night and they were looking seriously dishevelled. We were all just sitting there waiting for something to happen. It became obvious very quickly that she was expecting two families to arrive. She took one look at us and was not having it at all. Glen, being a travel agent, knew how to deal with her and make her stand by the booking because she was contractually bound to do so. He convinced her that the worst thing we would do to the villa was re-arrange the furniture. He told her that as a group of homosexual men, we were more likely to obsessively clean the place than trash it. She was very homophobic and extremely reluctant to have us staying in her stylish villa. She was not happy but she eventually agreed to give us a chance. We were playing ball, we reassured her that if anything was broken, we would pay for it. We told her she was welcome to come around to the villa any time to check on us.

Eventually we got the key to the place, jumped in the two hire cars and got to the villa, which was absolutely beautiful. The back of the house was made completely of glass, with stunning, unobstructed views of the ocean on all sides. The glass panels folded back, leading onto a fabulous terrace. It was bliss. But there were a lot of breakable objects in the place, and although most of us were not clumsy, Scott could break anything. Gary, who knew Scott very well, ordered us to get the bedrooms sorted out and get the breakables out of the place. We locked everything that was moveable and risked being broken into a cupboard because we knew what would happen if we didn't. Then we all picked our bedrooms. I always shared with Gary because we were best mates. Whether it was a double bed or twin beds we didn't care, we shared. Everyone else divided up the rooms. Nobody was going out with each other, we were all just mates.

We headed to the supermarket to buy food, and more alcohol of course. While we were busy filling trolleys we heard a high-pitched scream from the next aisle. We all dashed over to see what was going on.

There was Scott standing ashen over a pile of scattered white tablets. He had stashed a cigar tube of ecstasy in one of his orifices while travelling on the plane. Having taken the tube out when he got to the villa and put it in his pocket, he had forgotten all about it. He had two hundred ecstasy pills and the lid had come off the cigar case while we were in the supermarket and now they were all over the floor! There were never so many queens on their knees so fast, as we frantically gathered up the tablets. Meanwhile Scott, for the benefit of bemused shoppers, screamed, 'It's my medication, I need it for my holiday!' The hilarious mayhem had begun and it didn't stop for the whole week.

Every afternoon we went to bed about 4 PM to have a little nap, then we would get up and someone was assigned to cook dinner or we ate out. We had simple dishes, like a big bowl of pasta, salads and bread, and dinner was always followed by drinks on the terrace. It started off civilised, but as the nights wore on everybody got giddier and giddier. We usually hit Ibiza town, the old town, at about 10 PM. The place was fabulous; not too heavily commercialised, it was very cool and clubby.

We immersed ourselves in the club culture of Ibiza and it was really amazing to be around. There were a couple of guys from London who were living there for the summer, as well as a lot of Spanish and Italian people, so we got to know a good crowd. We had great connections and knew who to get our drugs from and where to get tickets for the big clubs. It was all about getting organised. We spent a lot of our days arranging what club we were going to that night, making sure we had tickets, arranging VIP passes or getting our names on the guest lists. We got everything organised, and then we got drunk. We waited until we got to the club to drop. We were going up and up and up all the time.

In the morning when the club was finished we either went on to another club called Space, which ran in the mornings until midday at the weekend, or headed straight to the beach. We peeled off the leather trousers, threw them into the boot of the car and put on our swimming trunks, as well as obligatory oversized sunglasses, and chilled out. We lay on the beach, had a joint, crashed out for an hour or two, and went for a swim. We woke up about lunch time to go to the bar and have a straightener – a beer and a sandwich – and then we were all ready to go again. The music on these beaches was always chilled, kick-back music and a little bit of Eighties stuff thrown in. It was very relaxing and allowed us to talk and share. It was these times, on a comedown on the beach, that I developed proper friendships and relationships with people, just sitting talking. It was those times that I loved. Once sunset came we were up and having cocktails again, of course. Then we planned dinner, who was going to cook, where we were going to go, what was on, what were we going to wear. And it all just started again. We did that for a week, in a different club every night. By the end of the weekend everybody knew us as 'those mad London boys'.

The rep arrived unannounced at our villa one evening. She said she had called around on a previous night and we had not been there. 'We were out darling, it is Ibiza,' we responded. It was mid-week and we were wrecked so we were in when she came to our door. We had a couple of friends around and we convinced her to stay for dinner. We wanted her to like us; we wanted to prove to her that homosexual men were not nasty or irresponsible. She had made it abundantly clear at the airport that she didn't want us there at all, but we still wanted her to like us. We begged her to stay and have dinner with us and she did. She was from Blackrock in Dublin so the lads threw me at her, being the nice Irish boy that I am. I was always willing to talk to anybody. She did end up liking us and when she realised that we had locked all the glass objects and breakables away, and that we had no intention of wrecking the place, she eased off.

On our last day in Ibiza we were in a heap, a shadow of our former selves. Our flight was early the next morning and some of us decided to have an early night. A few of the boys went into town for a bite to eat, while the rest of us stayed in the villa. I had had enough and went to bed. At about one o'clock in the morning Gary came into our room and was fumbling around in the dark. Lying there wondering to myself what was going on, I said 'Gar, what are you doing?'

'If you think for one second I'm going to stay in bed on our last night in Ibiza, you have got another thing coming. We've got two tickets for Amnesia, are you in or are you not?'

I couldn't believe he hadn't had enough – I was shattered. But if he was going then I was going. I was not going to miss out on anything. I had to work the next night in London, but I wasn't going to let that stop me. I jumped out of bed and pulled on a pair of jeans and off we went. We hadn't a lot of Spanish money left, but we still managed to have a fantastic night. We met up with all the people we had gotten to know on the island and together we went hell for leather for our last night. It was just fabulous. That night in the club the roof opened at dawn; it was 7.30 AM before we knew it. When the roof opened it was like we had gone to heaven with the sun blazing in. Everyone had sunglasses on and we were dancing like mad people. Our flight was at 9 AM, but we were having too much fun to care. The night before we had driven one of the cars into town, which was now needed to get everyone to the airport, but we didn't care – we just didn't want to stop dancing.

We got into the car to drive about twenty minutes back to the villa. On the way, we met the other boys on the road in the other car heading to the airport. There were six of them and their suitcases squashed into a tiny hatchback. They were furious of course. We drove past them and beeped the horn and kept going because we were so late. When we got back to the villa our cases were sitting outside the door. We didn't know what was in them or what had been left behind. The cleaners were already in the villa. We grabbed the cases, threw them in the boot of the car, and drove to the airport and dropped off the car. We were still buzzing from the drugs we took at the club. Furiously chewing gum, we checked in at the desk looking like two mad club bunnies. God knows what they thought of us standing there still in our club gear covered in sweat. We got changed in the bathroom in the airport still flying from the night before, all we could think about was getting a coffee, calming down and making sure we got on the flight.

By the time we got back to London it was late afternoon and I had to be at work by 6 PM. Knowing that I was working in a couple of hours and hadn't been to bed was not a good feeling. I had no sleep and I was beginning to crash. When I got into bed back in my apartment I couldn't sleep and I didn't want to take a sleeping tablet in case I didn't wake up in time for work, so I stayed up and took three caffeine tablets.

I went to work and managed a function. It was the longest night ever; I had the jitters, I was sweating, and I was pale. I really pushed it too hard. I ended up in bed for a week afterwards. The manger in the restaurant, of course, knew exactly what was going on and was laughing at me, knowing I was suffering badly. After that holiday I developed laryngitis, tonsillitis and a fever. My body was really beginning to say, *just stop*.

It all did stop, to a certain extent, in 1995 because I was so busy with work that I could no longer balance my job with my partying lifestyle. Clubbing took a back seat. It was in this year that the food and beverage director of the hotel I worked in got involved with Sir Terrance Conran and they were opening a restaurant called Mezzo, which was going to be the largest free-standing restaurant in Europe at the time. He suggested that I apply for a job as restaurant manager there, which I did. It was time for me to move, I had been in the hotel since 1988 and there was no possibility of promotion as the longstanding manager was staying put. I needed to develop my career some way, to seek out a new opportunity, so I moved and took the position of restaurant manager in Mezzo.

It was in the middle of Soho, which was my stomping ground. It was going to be a trendy place, an upmarket brasserie. My partying and drug taking didn't affect my job in the hotel because we planned our days off around a big clubbing weekend. I had a weekend off every three weeks so I planned my partying around that. I knew I couldn't do both when I went to Mezzo and I was able to stop everything without any trouble, it hadn't become an issue. The drinking still went on but it wasn't out of control, I was still hanging out with all my friends, I just stopped taking the drugs.

However, there was a party one weekend in the middle of Mezzo's busy opening period and I ended up going out on the Saturday night and found myself in Trade. Afterwards, I went back to somebody's house for a post-Trade barbecue on the Sunday morning. The person hosting the party gave all the guests champagne with a strawberry in it, and in each strawberry he had hidden a quarter of a tab of acid, unbeknownst to us. I ended up completely out of it. I was exhausted from work and it really sent me to a bad place but I had to get to work on Monday because I was giving staff training. I went into work after having very little sleep and I was a mess. I was in such a state I had to leave. Glen lived around the corner and I had to run around and get him to help me. My head was all over the place. He gave me a cold shower and a mug of coffee and talked to me for about an hour. I then went back into work and apologised to the manager, confessing that I had had a little bit of a panic attack. I did a whole training course with about twenty waiters. Apparently I was fantastic, but I was so out of it. Later, I rang the man who had hosted the party and let rip: 'If I lose my job over this I am going to kill you. How dare you do that to me?' My friends all knew how important this job was to me. They knew how hard I had worked to get it and how big this restaurant was going to be in London. I swore to myself after that day that this was never going to happen to me again, and the drugs stopped.

6

Mezzo

Frame every so-called disaster with these words: 'In five years, will this matter?'

The interviews for the position of restaurant manager in Mezzo were the toughest I had ever been through. There were four rounds and I was grilled by an intimidating panel, including John Torode, now a celebrity chef and presenter on BBC's *MasterChef*, and manager Wendy Hendricks, who is a very formidable character. She is feared by many, loathed by some and adored by most. It was more than a little daunting being questioned by them, but they had to ensure they got the best people for the job. The food and beverage manager in the Carlton Towers, David Loewi, who told me to apply for the job, believed in me and I had faith in myself. All my years of experience in hotels across the world had prepared me for this job and I knew I was ready.

Working in independent restaurants is a world apart from the hotel restaurant industry. The etiquette and attitude are very different. When I got the position, I was delighted with myself but frightened at the same time. I had landed a coveted job, one envied by everybody in the business, and I was at the height of my career. It was a huge move for me to go from hotels to an independent restaurant, as it was not so much about getting to know the clientele as about serving extremely high quality food to huge numbers of customers every day. Nothing could have prepared me for how stressful it was going to be, both physically and emotionally. I was jumping into the fire pit of hardcore restaurant work.

Conducting the interviews to find the perfect staff should have been an indication of what lay ahead. The other managers and I spent the summer interviewing hundreds of people for positions in a little office with no air conditioning on Wardour Street. The summer of 1995 was the one of the hottest on record. We had never had heat like it, and I was stuck in a tiny, sweltering office in stifling heat trying to find the best staff in the industry. We interviewed everyone two or three times to ensure we had the right people. The perspiration was constant and we worked six- or seven-day weeks before the opening. We were all completely drained after that process, and the restaurant hadn't even opened.

Mezzo was located in the middle of my stomping ground in Soho, in what used to be the famous Marquee Club. Spread over two levels, and sectioned off into a café, bar, mezzanine level and restaurant, Mezzo could seat almost one thousand people at any time. It was a spectacularly impressive building with a two-storey restaurant. There were two kitchens, both of which were situated behind a glass wall so that customers could see in during service There was a fabulous *Titanic*-style staircase in the middle of the building connecting both floors. The restaurant I managed was in the basement level and seated 350 people at 100 tables. It also had live jazz music at weekends and was open until 3 AM. Sir Terence Conran owned the restaurant and Mezzo was part of his ever-expanding restaurant portfolio in London. Mezzo was his new project and it was the most talked about restaurant in the city at that time. It was the late 1990s, the beginning of widespread economic boom, and fabulous, nightclub-style restaurants were opening at a phenomenal rate all over the city. It was a very exciting time for the industry and it was amazing to be a part of it.

The explosion of exclusive restaurants opening in London in 1995 – 2,500 restaurant seats opened within three months – included the Atlantic Bar and Grill, Oxo Tower, Blue Bird, Avenue and Titanic, to name a few. However, the one everyone was excited about was Mezzo. It was the biggest and by far the busiest. The buzz around the opening of Mezzo was electric. Everyone who was anyone was waiting in anticipation for the doors to open and the hype was palpable. There was a massive PR drive, with articles about the opening in every magazine and newspaper for weeks. Everyone wanted a table at Mezzo. The build-up and preparation for the opening took its toll on all of us; we were exhausted, but also elated.

There was a soft opening in September of that year, where people were offered lunch at half price. This lasted for three days, and was then extended to a dinner service, also for a couple of nights, which catered for 200 covers. It was like a trial run to see what hitches and problems would be encountered when all our planning was put into practice. It was a way of seeing what could go wrong and gave us a chance to rectify the problems. And as customers were getting their meals at knock-down prices, they didn't complain if everything didn't run smoothly. The second opening was for invited food writers and critics and that was an extremely pressurised night. It was nerve-racking. There was no room for error – we had to ensure these invited guests had the best food and service to guarantee glowing reviews. The experience they had in Mezzo had to match the hype around the restaurant. We had to deliver, and we did. I was running around that restaurant like a blue-arsed fly ensuring everything went to plan and all the staff were doing everything correctly. It was a great success but it was the toughest build-up and opening I have ever done.

When the doors of the restaurant properly opened, people came flocking to Mezzo to taste the food and experience dining in this magnificent restaurant. There really was no restaurant like it in London at that time and everyone wanted a reservation. I took control of the restaurant and it was like driving a jumbo jet. I had eighty staff under me in total, including twenty-two head waiters, twenty-two waiters and twenty-two runners, ten hostesses and about eight bar staff. The management team consisted of four first head waiters or floor managers, two assistant managers and the manager. I needed every bit of my energy and concentration to know what was happening in the kitchen and on the floor at all times, as well as ensuring that all customers were getting food on time and tables were turning according to the bookings. It was a beautiful restaurant when it was empty but when it was full of people, it became a monster. I had to tame that monster; learn the system to control it. We had four operators answering the phones only, constantly taking reservations; two runners were allocated to serve bread and butter only all night, which was unheard of before. It was the place in London to go to; the hottest ticket in town.

Mezzo's client list was a melting pot of business people, socialites and celebrities. Record companies like Sony and EMI were just up the road from the restaurant, so I was constantly getting calls from their management asking for a table for world-class performers. Celine Dion came into the restaurant one night with her record company for dinner. I was so busy running around the floor, controlling my monster, that I simply hadn't time to make a huge fuss over her. As I raced around the tables, making sure everything was running as close to clockwork as possible in such a packed, high-octane restaurant, I could feel someone watching me closely. I felt eyes following my every move and when I turned around Celine Dion was staring at me intently. I caught her eyes and she gave me a beaming grin, as I did to her. She just gave me the thumbs up. Someone so successful, with such a strong work ethic was impressed with the level at which I was working. It was like she identified my passion. I was delighted with myself.

Mariah Carey's people also rang late one night looking for a table for her. We were booked out and the place was crazy, but of course I told them it was no problem; I would juggle something and would have a table for her within half an hour. I frantically rearranged seating plans to get her PA the table she wanted, made arrangements for her to come in through the kitchen so she wouldn't be mobbed, got my top waiters prepped to serve her and warned the kitchen she was coming, in case she had any specific food requirements. It was manic that night. After making sure everything was in place she came in the back door of the restaurant with a massive entourage. Then she ordered a bowl of chips . . . I felt like screaming at her. A bowl of bloody chips! I was disgusted. The least she could have done after all our effort was to actually order a delicious meal off the menu. When the chefs were told what she wanted, they were less than impressed. She could have just as easily gone to a chippy down the road, where she could have had a battered burger to go with her chips.

I was in every day at 10 AM, or 4 PM for the evening shift, and worked until 4 AM. On weeknights we served up to 600 people and on Friday and Saturday nights we did 900 covers – turning tables three times, which was a nightmare to manage. This element of the trade was new to me and I had to adapt to customers only having a set amount of time to dine and then vacating the table for the next sitting. In hotel restaurants it was unheard of to ask clientele to leave a table. I was used to a more customer-orientated etiquette, but in Mezzo it was about numbers coming through the door. I had to get people in, ensure they were served starter, main course and dessert with coffee and be gone within the hour and three-quarter limit, then reset the table for the next sitting. When people reserved a table for 7 PM they were told when making the booking that they would have to leave by 8.45 PM. Asking people to leave a table went completely against the grain, the opposite of what I had learned, but I had to do it. Most people didn't mind at all, as they knew this was the case when making the reservation, and I didn't take no for an answer. One of my favourite lines was, 'I know it's annoying, but that's what we do here and everyone is told when making a reservation.

So I don't want you to destroy a perfectly good evening so just follow me to the bar, enjoy the music and have a night cap or two.'

The food in Mezzo was brilliant and it had a real party atmosphere. Between the music and over a thousand people chatting, laughing, shouting and drinking, the noise was immense. But as everyone else enjoyed themselves, I was running myself into the ground. The pressure was like nothing I had experienced before. It was non-stop trying to ensure that all members of staff were doing what they should be. I regularly had blisters on my feet from running around on the marble floor and my head was constantly pounding. In its first year, the restaurant turned over something crazy like £50,000 a day, and it was open seven days a week, so it was making approximately £350,000 a week.

My way of dealing with the pressure was to kiss goodbye to mister nice guy and become a bitch on the floor. I didn't take crap from anybody, be it staff or customers, and some nights the restaurant was more like a battleground. With 900 covers a night it was inevitable there would be some complaints. If even just 10 percent of customers were not satisfied, it meant I had to deal with ninety disgruntled customers' complaints. I learnt very quickly how to suss out a genuine complaint and handle it very well; and also to know when someone was trying to pull a fast one.

With the loud, heady atmosphere in the restaurant, customers sometimes got caught up with it all and started behaving strangely. One particularly busy night I found myself pinned up against the wall by a male customer with his hands wrapped around my throat. It was 8.45 PM and it was time to vacate the table he was at with several other people.

He insisted he was not ready to go, but I firmly told him that was the policy and he was aware of it when he sat down to eat. He got very irate and the next thing I knew he was on his feet assaulting me. I was initially shocked but then the adrenalin kicked in and I kneed him in the balls. He wasn't long freeing me from his grasp and I managed to throw him out of the restaurant without any more outbursts. Incidents like that stay with you and chip away at the coat of armour. That was the last time I allowed a customer to treat me like that and I became determined to defend myself. I had no qualms about telling people to get out of my restaurant. I would be told, 'I'm taking your name', and my response was always: 'You can take everyone's name if you want, but you are not getting any dinner here tonight. Now get out!'

I dealt with every complaint in the book while I worked there, and people never ceased to amaze me. Another night there was a guy at a table of ten and, after polishing of his fillet steak and leaving the plate clean of any food, he called me over and presented me with a black stone he claimed was in his meat. Of course I investigated every serious complaint, so I took the stone to the chef. We discussed and looked at all possibilities. The area where the deliveries were left was covered in plain white concrete cement, there was no charcoal on the grill and the kitchen was completely tiled front door to back door and spotless. We would have sold a hundred fillet steaks that night so we knew if there had been a problem with one there would have been a problem with more. I knew this particular customer was trying to pull a fast one. I couldn't say that to him, but there was no way I was letting him away with it either. I returned to his table and placed the stone in front of him and politely but firmly told him we believed it had not come from our restaurant. As a gesture of good will, I was willing to take the cost of his meal and the bottles of champagne his party had been drinking off the bill, which came to over £1,000. But he was adamant he was not paying for anything. I told him there was no way he was getting everything for free and he must pay the bill once the reduction of what I was offering was taken off it. He got very aggressive and was screaming at me in the middle of restaurant, causing a proper scene. I simply cleared everything of the table and told him if he was not satisfied with what I was offering him he could write a letter of complaint to the general manager, which was our policy, but he was not leaving my restaurant without paying his bill. In the end I had no choice but to call the police. This individual was so irrational and downright stubborn that we were all in the restaurant with two police officers until 5 AM. I was not backing down, he was either going to pay his bill or I was going to see him in court over it. Eventually, after hours of heated arguments chaired by the Metropolitan Police, he parted with his money.

Although it was a much sought-after place to work, Mezzo chewed staff up and spat them out at an alarming rate. We haemorrhaged waiters who found that they simply couldn't take the pace and perform to such a high standard day after day, and I was constantly interviewing for new staff. The management were also dropping like flies. After just two months one assistant manager couldn't take any more and left, while another ended up in hospital. I never ate properly as there was no staff food like in the hotels. I had to run out and grab a sandwich from Pret a Manger or somewhere close by and eat it on the move. One saving grace was that, at night, I allowed managers to order a meal from the kitchen. The hours I was working and the stress I was under was very dangerous for my health and I became very thin. I personally suffered for the job, it took so much out of me and there was very little left. My personal life was an absolute mess. The restaurant was only open three months when the exhaustion really hit me. One night, after another hectic shift, I was sitting on a high stool at the bar at 4 AM with my dry cleaning in my hand, waiting for a taxi to take me home. Someone said my cab was there and I literally couldn't get out of the chair, I was so exhausted. It took everything in me to just stand up and take those few steps to that taxi. I cried that night in the cab.

Mezzo was so loud and chaotic that when I had any free time I didn't want to go to restaurants, pubs or bars. I just wanted peace and quiet and definitely no crowds. The only time I saw my friends really was when they came to Mezzo for dinner. They loved that they could call me and get a table in one of the best restaurants in London at short notice. My friends watched me work non-stop but I didn't let them see the damage it was doing to me. On the very rare occasions I did go out with them, they were always very impressed that I could get a table for us practically anywhere in the city, as people that had left Mezzo were now scattered in restaurants throughout London.

But ultimately I became a hermit, hiding out in my apartment drinking by myself. On my days off I just slept, ate, drank alcohol, slept a bit more and then went back to work again. I worked every Saturday night and never got home before 5 AM. I crawled out of bed on Sunday about midday, wrecked. I couldn't switch off, and I reran the previous night's shift over and over again; a rundown of the complaints, the tables and the orders. The noise of the restaurant was constantly in my head. I would sit with a mug of coffee, trying to eat something for breakfast but I couldn't find any peace. All I wanted to do was to block it out, which I found I could only do with a drink. I usually poured myself a large glass of wine, quite often accompanied by a Valium, in an attempt to calm down and unwind. And of course once I opened a bottle of wine, I always finished it and there was another one chilling in the fridge. The job consumed my life. Gary had been at home in Australia for a couple of months and when he returned to London he came to visit me. When I opened the door to him he just froze, and the look of horror on his face terrified me. I was down to about 60 kilos; my face was ashen white and there were heavy black marks under my eyes. I was a shadow of my old self.

The stress was so immense at times it paralysed me. There were occasions when I woke up in the morning and just couldn't face going into work. I lay in bed unable to move and couldn't cope with the thought of returning to the roaring wild beast that was Mezzo. The anxiety was horrendous. I would ring my manager and tell him I couldn't take it any more and I was leaving. He always talked me off the ledge and told me to take a couple of days to get myself back together and to return when I felt fit enough. After a couple of days I always went back. My general manager understood the stress we were under because he saw it firsthand. I was good at my job and they didn't want to lose me, but my life was spiralling into a whirlpool of work and drinking just to cope with the job. I was having a mini breakdown but didn't recognise it.

Every Monday night I took the staff out and got them drunk. Like me, they worked incredibly hard and we all needed to blow off steam. We went to Break for the Border in Soho, which was open until 4 AM and had two-for-one drink offers, so we got hammered. We went out together at least one other night during the week too; we all understood each other and what we were going through and found it difficult to be around 'normal' people with nine-to-five jobs. We downed drinks to stop us from exploding under the pressure of working in Mezzo. When we went out we were crazy and partied until the small hours. We were constantly running on adrenalin and drinking was our way of escaping the pressure. Finishing a shift in Mezzo was like being an actor coming off-stage with the buzz of the performance still coursing through your veins.

I resented that I was working so hard and the job had consumed my life. I loved my job and I knew I was at the height of my career, but I also hated it. It was having a devastating effect on me but I just kept doing it because I was determined not to fail. I wouldn't give up, even though it was killing me. Letting go of my position was not an option; I was disposable and there was a long line of people who would be happy to take my place. But I was exhausted. Generally, it is understood in the industry that jobs like mine have an expiry date of eighteen months to two years. That is as long as anyone should remain in an environment with that level of intensity. But I kept going in Mezzo for four years. I was exhausted but I was afraid of what my next step would be if I left. There was nowhere left for me to go in London better than Mezzo.

Eventually, worn out and fed up, I started going for interviews for different jobs in the hope of finding a way out, but the people interviewing me saw straight away that I was completely burnt out and badly in need of a break. Then, like a gift from the gods, a man offered me a job in Dublin at La Stampa. He promised me the sun, moon and stars with a salary I just couldn't refuse. He made me the offer in February 1999 and by 25 March, I was back in Ireland. I resigned from Mezzo, had a leaving party, got on a plane and suddenly found myself living back home in Naas. I believe there was somebody up there looking after me because I was a mess and so grateful to be escaping London. The restaurant was a huge success and it was amazing for me professionally. Having Mezzo on my CV was like a golden ticket for many years. It opened so many doors, but it nearly killed me. For years afterwards I often woke up sweating from a nightmare about being back on the floor in Mezzo.

7

Back in Ireland

*If we threw our problems in a pile and saw everyone else's,
we'd grab ours back.*

– Regina Brett

I was delighted to be home in Ireland, away from the gruelling workload of Mezzo and the endless nights of boozing. It was March 1999 and I went to stay at my parents' house in Naas for a little while to figure out what my next step was going to be. It was lovely to be back in the family home; it was so calm and quiet compared to my hectic lifestyle in London. But I was in limbo, the only real certainty I had in my life was the job in La Stampa. I was starting the new position on the first week of April, so I set about trying to establish a new life in Dublin and went hunting for somewhere to live. I found a lovely little one-bedroom apartment on Pembroke Road, which was within walking distance of the restaurant. Being able to stroll into work rather than the chaotic commutes during rush hour to my job in London was heaven. But being back in Dublin was also strange; so much had changed in the city since the last time I had lived there. I had been away from Dublin for so long that, in many ways, I had to rediscover the city.

The last time I lived there was when I was in college. My college years were some of the happiest of my life and the city had been part of that, a great place for adventures with my friends. But now I had a lot more experience under my belt. I was thirty-five years of age and I was returning to a place that I had last known in my youth. It was a very strange experience and very lonely in many ways. On my previous visits back to Dublin, they were generally weekends full of partying and staying in hotels, but now I had to re-build my life here and it was difficult. I had spent so long being this party animal workaholic, surrounded by fabulous friends, and now I found myself back in Ireland not knowing many people. I had left the whirlwind lifestyle in London that had distracted me from how I was feeling and had successfully kept buried what had happened to me in my past. Back in Dublin, there were fewer distractions, fewer diversions and I was forced to address some of the things I had kept hidden for so long. It was a crossroads in my life.

On my first day of work in La Stampa I went through the restaurant door and there was nobody there to meet me, show me the ropes or brief me on what was expected of me in my role. I stood there in the restaurant not knowing what I was supposed to be doing; I didn't even know what my job title was meant to be. The owner had gone to Spain for three weeks and I was left flying solo, so I did what I always do and threw myself into my work. I just got in and got on with it. The assistant manager was a charismatic young gentleman with a great sense of humour called Declan Maxwell, who is still in the restaurant business today. I think we were made from the same mould and we quickly became good friends. He had a conscientious attitude to work, a similar personality and we found the same things funny. Having been in the restaurant scene in Dublin for a couple of years when I met him, Declan knew everybody in the industry and had lots of friends. I didn't know anybody really and was like a fish out of water but he ensured me I would build up a circle of friends and work network within six months, and he was right. He was a rock for me while I tried to establish a life in Dublin.

Since the owner was not there, I started running the restaurant as I saw fit. The place needed work, so I put together a whole rejuvenation programme to try and build the business up, because it was clear to me it was beginning to slip. It was a beautiful old building but it needed a little bit of a modern twist to bring it back to its former glory. I began slightly renovating the place and working on the interior design of the restaurant, without a designer. I added a bit of flair and it was fabulous. The chef was a friend of mine from London who had worked in Mezzo and was instrumental in me being offered the job in La Stampa. We worked together to create a modern, mouth-watering menu that both of us were proud to offer our customers. Between us, we had a lot of experience in some of the best restaurants in the world, and we knew what we were doing. But when the owner came back from Spain he did not like the changes. He didn't appreciate what I was doing, the hard work I had put into regenerating his business. I had arranged for a launch to be held in the restaurant one night before it was open for customers to dine. It was a great PR exercise, which was good for the restaurant's reputation, but he didn't see it that way. A number of issues had been building up and we ended up having a rather heated argument. We parted company very quickly and on extremely bad terms. I had only been in the job six weeks but I left. I was completely horrified by the way he had treated me; I always had pride in my work and for someone to attack me like that when I was feeling vulnerable really affected me. Leaving a job under such a terrible black cloud really knocked my self-esteem. I was very fragile after working to the point of exhaustion in London and this destroyed me a little bit more.

After that experience I took three months out of work. It was the first time since I was a teenager that I had not worked; even through college I always held down a job, and with every position I was ever in I worked until I was about to collapse. But now I found myself with no job, the one thing that had been a constant in my life up to now. My job had defined who I was to a certain degree, and prevented me from thinking about my demons, and without it I crumbled. I spent that summer just hovering over no man's land; I didn't know what to do or who I was any more. I was in a really bad place and I retreated even further into myself, locking myself away from the world. I had no meaning or direction in my life and I was totally lost.

I spent a lot of time in the country in either my sister Mary's place or my parents' house, doing things like cutting the grass and other odd jobs just to pass the hours and fill in the days. I didn't know where I should be or where I wanted to be. I didn't know where my home was any more or who I was, really. I started to drink heavily and it spiralled out of control very quickly. At the time I thought it was fine, but it was dangerous. I was very hurt and I didn't know how to deal with it, so I drank a lot on my own. It was the first time that problems from my past, the abuse I had suffered, which I had buried deep inside me, began to surface because there was no work to distract me from the painful images of my past; I was just left with me. I didn't know who I was at all, and I had no idea how to find myself again, or discover a new me. I had been used to being part of a close-knit circle of friends that looked after each other and picked each other up when we were down. We laughed together through the great times and helped each other through the bad times. But now that support system was gone. I was falling and I felt like there was nobody there to catch me. It was sociably acceptable to roll around the pubs in Ireland very drunk on your own, and that is what I did on occasions. Nobody batted an eyelid at someone sitting in a bar on their own downing gin and tonics before stumbling home. Also, as I lived on my own, when I shut the front door of my apartment behind me nobody knew how many bottles of wine or gin and tonics I went through sitting there alone. The more I drank on my own, the more memories of my childhood resurfaced and the more difficult it became to deal with life and the real world. They were three dark months.

I decided the best way to get myself out of the abyss I was falling further into was to get a job. I needed a purpose; a direction to follow. However, there were no jobs in Dublin that appealed to me. I was on the verge of going back to London, when in September, I got a job with a company called Master Chefs that was opening in the Mansion House. My role was to work at their functions in the Mansion House and organise catering at the horse racing events across the country. It was a far cry from Mezzo and the Rib Room, there was no glamour or glitz, but I hoped it would pull me out of the rut I was stuck in. It was great fun at times and the people I worked with were brilliant, but I absolutely detested the functions and hated serving in the suites of race courses or outdoors. I had worked in a five-star hotel and a one of the best restaurants in London, and here I was wrapping sandwiches at Fairyhouse Racecourse in -2 degrees wearing a Gucci tie and a Cartier watch. It was not good. It was not that I was being snobby about doing the job, it was just not where I wanted to be, it was not how I imagined my life would turn out. When I was charming the rich and famous in exclusive restaurants in London I never dreamt this would be what I would end up doing. I left that job and took a part-time position in the Central Hotel serving breakfast, which I hated equally as much. I didn't stay in that job very long either. I was in hell and my drinking continued and I began to feel even worse about how my life was going. I knew something had gone wrong; I had taken a wrong turn on the path of my life. I didn't know what I was meant to do to fix it but I knew I had to get myself together. I decided I had to find a job in Ireland that I loved and wanted to do, something that when I got up in the morning I didn't dread going to , or I was going back to London. I missed my life in London in many ways, but deep down I knew that if I went back there, it could be even more destructive than staying in Ireland.

I met up with some of my friends from college who were living in Dublin. I went to the opening of the Morrison Hotel and some of them were there. They all knew how much I was struggling to cope with finding my place in the world again. We were chatting away and I told them that I didn't know what I was doing back in Ireland and that I was seriously considering going back to London. One of them was Michael Brennan, who had been in my class, and his brother was general manager of the Four Seasons. Michael knew I was not coping and told me to go and talk to his brother, not necessarily to get a job, but even for some advice. I rang him and arranged to meet him and we had a long, long conversation about restaurants, hotels, my career, what I wanted to do, where I wanted to go and how I could do it. He was a great help and gave me insight into how to piece my life back together work-wise. There were jobs going in the Four Seasons and he suggested that I apply for the role of restaurant manager.

Everybody was talking about the new five-star hotel coming to Dublin that was going to be the place to go, anybody that was anybody was waiting in anticipation for the opening. At that point I wasn't sure whether I wanted to go back to the five-star hotel world or to remain a part of the independent restaurant scene, as they represent two very different challenges. But I knew that with my experience I could do the job extremely well. I applied for the position and got it. The high-end hotel industry was what I knew best and I was delighted to be returning to that environment. I may not have known where my home was, who I really was any more, or how I was going to confront my past, but I did know how to do this job to a very high standard. I had found a place where I could flourish.

Right: My First Holy
Communion

Below: My sister and me at
the strawberry patch

Left: Restaurant manager on duty in the
Rib Room of the Carlton Tower
Hotel, London

Below: Trying on the New Year's Eve hats
with Gary at the Rib Room
in 1991

All the team at the Rib Room, New Year's Eve 1991

Mezzo Restaurant in London, where I worked from 1995 to 1999

Ibiza with the boys in 1994

Left: Gay Pride in London, 1992

Below: A visit from Gary in New York, June 1990

There's not much to do on Fire Island when the sun don't shine!

Above: Filming *The Restaurant* with
guest chef Joe Duffy

Right: Wrapping another series of
The Restaurant in 2011
with director Regina
Looby

Above: The fundraiser lunch at Pichet with Elaine Normile and my sister Mary

Left: ISPCC lunch in the Four Seasons with Maria Collins and friends

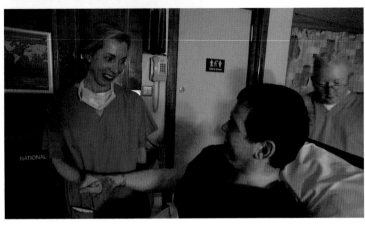

Going to theatre for my transplant accompanied by Zita Lalor, March 2012. Image © RTÉ

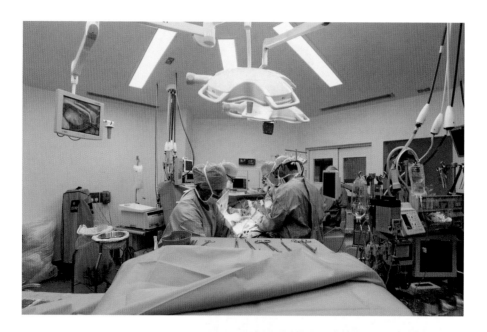

Above: The transplant operation in progress. Image © RTÉ

Right: The day I left hospital after my heart transplant

With Gary in London, September 2012

Mum, Dad, Mary, Tim and the kids pictured at Mary's 40th
birthday party

8

Realisation and the Road to Recovery

We are not human beings having a spiritual experience; we are spiritual beings having a human experience.
– Pierre Teilhard de Chardin

Once I had made up my mind to accept the position as manager in the restaurant of the Four Seasons, I knew it was the right thing to do. I needed time for myself. I was familiar with how the restaurant operated and knew I could shine there. I was excited about getting back on a restaurant floor, being part of the buzz and interacting with clientele again. But that was not how it worked out. The opening of the hotel was delayed and instead of being back in the familiar sphere of a bustling restaurant, I found myself stuck in an office behind a desk. This was not my idea of fun; in fact, it was my hell.

I don't do desk jobs very well. I get irritable if I have to sit too long in front of a computer. It was monotonous and gave me too much time to think. I was edgy and the memories of my abuse plagued me day and night. There was no relief as I was not busy enough to distract myself from my thoughts. The only way I could escape was through alcohol. My new job was meant to save me from the demons of my childhood, but instead I had long, empty hours to think.

Every morning I came into work and sat behind my desk, watching the clock, counting down to the time when it would be acceptable to go for lunch and have a drink. I always had a long, boozy lunch before returning to the office for a couple of hours. Come 5 PM, I was more than likely back sitting in a bar downing gin and tonics, followed by more drinks in my apartment. The nights that I didn't go to a bar I drank on my own at home. Every morning I woke up with a muzzy head, went to work and did it all over again. It was a very lonely place to be.

The management of the Four Seasons knew there was nothing for the staff to do now that the opening of the hotel had been delayed, so we were all loaned out to other hotels within the international chain that needed help. And I couldn't believe my luck when myself and two others were told we were going to the Beverly Wilshire Hotel on Rodeo Drive in Los Angeles. Talk about landing in fabulosity! Only a couple of months previous, I was serving grub in the rain at the races, and now I was going to glamorous, sunny LA, where all the beautiful people live – thank you, God! Two colleagues and I happily packed our bags and headed off for three months.

When we first arrived at the Beverly Wilshire, we were given a suite to stay in. It was pure luxury and I loved it. It definitely beat sitting in an office all day. When the hotel started to get busy we were moved into one of the penthouse apartments in the tower of the hotel. A renowned radio host used to live in the apartment that became our new home. The penthouse was 1970s kitsch at its best, with all the original décor still intact. The 1,500 square foot penthouse on the eighteenth floor had a wrap-around balcony and we really felt quite special living there.

When I first saw my bedroom, I couldn't believe it. I felt like I had walked into a Bond movie. There was a massive bed on a pedestal in the middle of the room with a mirrored headboard and mirrored ceiling. The ensuite bathroom had a sauna, a Jacuzzi and also had mirrored floors, walls, and ceiling. There really was no way of escaping my reflection in that place. There was also a walk-in wardrobe the size of some flats I had lived in and in the main living area there were two double beds where the girls slept, sofas, a TV and a kitchenette. We couldn't believe our luck. We were living like queens!

When it came to work all three of us hit the ground running; we were full of energy after being stuck sitting in an office for three months, and were itching to get back doing what we excelled at. I was put into the lounge and restaurant and I loved being back in that environment. We were all Four Seasoned-up, as we had been trained into their systems, ethos and culture. We had it all going on – we were young, dynamic and eager to work hard and people around us fed off our enthusiasm. Our lust for life and hunger for work motivated the staff quite a lot and I could see the energy throughout the hotel that we brought with us.

It was great fun working there and being in LA on Rodeo Drive had a real sense of glamour. There are so many celebrities in LA that no one really batted an eyelid when someone mega-famous was about. I was up at 4.30 AM every morning and downstairs by 5 AM, with breakfast served an hour later. The doors opened at 6 AM sharp every morning and initially I could not believe the amount of people up and about at that time. Back in Dublin most people were still fast asleep or just coming home from a night out at six in the morning. But in LA, people were full of energy and chatting excitedly from first light.

I didn't mind getting up that early as LA is beautiful at that time in the morning. All the big casting agents for Hollywood came to the restaurant for breakfast meetings on a daily basis. It's a cliché, but it's true to say that everybody in LA wants to be famous – that's why they are there. Waiters and bar staff described themselves as out-of-work actors and everybody was constantly going to castings and auditions in the hope of becoming rich and famous. There was a real buzz and excitement around the place; everyone believed that their dreams were going to come true.

One afternoon at lunch we had a table of ten, comprising one man and nine women, who all looked like to be in their forties. I was intrigued by this man, decked out in a Chanel suit and managing to charm so many attentive ladies at once. A work colleague later informed me that he was a surgeon and the women, who were his clients, were in reality closer to seventy or eighty. On closer examination I could see it was a posse of elderly women who looked flawlessly beautiful. Only in America! There was the young glamorous gang who frequented the hotel, but there was also the older Hollywood, Beverly Hills set. There were a lot of glamorous pensioners too, wearing designer clothes and big sunglasses, in wheelchairs or shuffling around on Zimmer frames. Most of them had had plastic surgery and looked much younger than their age, which was only revealed when you had to shout because they couldn't hear you properly, or they asked for a straw to drink their tea.

When we were not working, we were partying. The three of us didn't know each other very well at the beginning but we quickly became firm friends, working, socialising and living together. We didn't have to cook our own food as room service was delivered to the penthouse. And, of course, the off-licence was around the corner and it sold vodka by the gallon-load. We were able to buy two and a half litre jugs of the stuff. We couldn't really afford to go out that much because we were all still paying rent at home, so we had our own parties in the penthouse. The litres of booze would usually lead to hilarious conversations and dancing around the sitting room. We might have been broke a lot of the time, but we still managed to have a ball, thanks to the jugs of vodka and good company.

As I had to start work so early it meant I had to begin drinking early. If I was going to get drunk, which I usually did, it had to happen before 9 PM so I could get enough hours' sleep before my alarm went off at 4.30 AM. I spent my time in LA working really hard and getting drunk. I was eating all the wrong food, drinking cocktails and vodka every night and doing no exercise, so my weight ballooned. During those three months, heavy drinking started to really become part of my life, it became the norm.

The management of the Beverly Wilshire sent us to Vegas on our last weekend in America to thank us for all our hard work before we went home. They arranged for a limousine to bring us to the airport and we flew to Vegas. We were given a huge suite overlooking the main strip. The other Four Season staff from Dublin who had been working in other hotels in the US were treated to a weekend in Vegas too and we all met up, delighted to exchange stories of our time in America. That weekend in Vegas was wild to say the least. The two girls and I arrived at 8 AM and went straight to the casino. We didn't have the money to do any serious gambling so we stayed away from the roulette table, focusing instead on the slot machines. We started drinking early that day. I got so drunk that I missed out on the first night in Vegas.

After having a skinful I decided I had to go to bed, but I was so drunk I couldn't find my room. I spent ages wandering around corridors, completely lost. Eventually I ended up where I had started – in the bar.

I staggered into the lounge and one of my friends had to lead me back to my room and put me to bed. I was a mess. I was in Vegas and all I was fit to do was pass out in a hotel room. In bed that night, in my drunken stupor, I was so sick. I knew then I had completely overdone it with alcohol. It was the first time I regretted something I had done because of drink. The next morning as I lay in bed with a pounding headache, trying to piece together what had happened the night before, I realised for the first time I had an alcohol problem. I was bloated and out of control. My life was chaotic and I spent most of it lost in a haze of drunkenness and hangovers. That was the first time I thought that something had to be done about my drinking. But I didn't stop; I spent the rest of the weekend partying and put the idea that I had a drink problem out of my head. I was not ready to deal with it.

We went back to LA exhausted after the weekend. We only had three days left before we returned to Dublin so we decided to make the most of the LA scene and went out every night. The morning of the flight back home I woke up in a hotel room and there was a girl in the bed beside me. It was one of the managers of the hotel and we had gotten so drunk that I was incapable of getting back to my room so we fell asleep in the same bed. I couldn't remember how I got there. I had the hangover from hell. It was just horrendous. I was horrendous. I just couldn't get myself together; I couldn't function. The flight was at 11 AM and I had not even packed my bag. I tried everything to make myself human again – coffee, water and headache tablets – but nothing helped. I tried to cram my clothes into a suitcase but I just couldn't cope so I left half of my stuff behind me and got the flight in the clothes that I had slept in. One of the guys that worked in the restaurant saw how panicked I was and gave me two Xanax in an attempt to calm me down. I had to endure an eleven-hour flight and the only way I could get through it was to have a couple of drinks to knock myself out again and sleep. I arrived back in Dublin dishevelled and half-drunk. My mother was at the airport to meet me. I took one look at her face and saw how disappointed she was and how horrified she was at the state of me; of what I had become.

I returned to work in the Four Seasons but the hotel was still not ready to open. I weighed fifteen stone, which was not a good look for a gay man, and I was constantly ill from alcohol. The hotel was not opening until February and I was back to being stuck in an office every day. I had too much time on my hands so I filled it with drinking. My life was falling apart at the seams and cracks were really beginning to appear. I was spiralling further into the murky world of alcoholism. I went back to taking long lunches that involved more gin and tonics than food, and when I got home I had cocktails or bottles of wine. I was drinking every night; I was in the pub three nights a week and drinking on my own the rest of the time. Things were getting really bad but I didn't know how to stop it.

Because I was drinking every night, I struggled to get out of bed in the morning, so I was regularly late for work. I got away with it to a certain extent but I was being watched from the sidelines and people at work were beginning to notice the change in me, in my attitude and my behaviour. I was in a demoralised state; I had a lack of interest in myself personally and in things around me. It was becoming very clear to everyone but me that I had an alcohol problem.

With the permission of my bosses at the Four Seasons, I took a part-time job at weekends in Diep Le Shaker on Pembroke Street. I wanted to keep myself busy and fill the hours that I was spending drinking with something else. I hoped it would get me into a routine that didn't revolve around alcohol. I worked in the Four Seasons during the week and in the restaurant at the weekends, but I didn't really give a damn about the part-time job. Before going to work in the restaurant I was tipping away at alcohol. I often made excuses to leave early and went home and just drank more. It was a bad time for me. The only thing I really cared about was drinking. When you drink as much alcohol as I was at that time, you lose interest in everything completely – your work, your family, your friends, your appearance – and all you care about is your next drink.

I rang my boss in the restaurant one day and told him I couldn't make it into work because I had the flu. But that night, one of my colleagues was having a party to celebrate her birthday and I arrived to it rotten drunk. Everyone from work, including my boss, was there, but I didn't care. I was losing a grasp on reality. At one of my lowest points I spent three days drinking solidly at home alone. I stayed in the same clothes the whole time and just drank until I passed out. When I came around I just started drinking again. The days merged into one big long, lonely drinking session. In the end I had to ring my sister Mary to come up and get me out of the house because I couldn't leave it, I was in such a bad state.

I didn't even party any more. I had no interest in socialising or meeting people, I just wanted to isolate myself from everything and everyone. I locked myself away from the rest of the world and downed bottles of vodka, gin and wine. It was the first time I was truly on my own, because I didn't have friends around me like I had in London. It was just me and the demons in my head and they were not good company. I had no other coping mechanisms. I got to the point where I didn't care about anything except getting drunk; I was wild. I had lost interest in everything, my motivations, ambition and drive had gone, my personality was beginning to suffer and I looked dreadful. I had hit rock bottom and I was not able to hide it any more.

A colleague at the Four Seasons, who was a friend of mine that I had worked with in London, saw the problem I had and was the first person to approach me about it. She recognised that I was at a point where I needed help and she took me aside at work one day and told me I had to do something about my drinking. She pointed out to me that I was the first to go to the pub if anyone mentioned going for a drink and because I was hungover all the time, I was not doing my job properly. I was horrified that someone was talking about my alcohol problem to me out loud because no one had done that before. As long as nobody was saying it to me I could pretend what I was doing was alright. She backed me into a corner and of course I got defensive and denied I had a problem with alcohol and refused the help she was offering me. But she was not prepared to accept that and went to the management in the hotel about my problem. Of course they were already aware of it. Management gave me an ultimatum: either get help with my alcohol problem or lose my job. I was turning up late for work every day and I was beginning to break all the rules. I realised I simply could not get away with it any more. In one sense I was angry, but deep down I was relieved that the game was up. I agreed to go to rehab. That day I went to a GP across the road from the hotel and she recommended a five-week detox programme in St Patrick's University Hospital. I had seen people close to me go through the process before so I knew how it worked. I was terrified; facing up to my problems was like admitting failure. I was ashamed. My pride and my self-esteem were shattered. It was very difficult to confront my problem head on, but it had to be done.

On Valentine's Day 2001, I checked into St Pat's Hospital. My colleague came with me for moral support. I was still very angry with her for putting me in the position I found myself in. I blamed her, but I was still glad that someone had heard my cry for help. Walking through the doors of the hospital, I was terrified at the prospect of not being allowed to drink. I didn't know what to expect or what lay ahead of me. But I was at the point that I did want help and I was ready to tackle the problem, no matter how tough it was going to get.

I was shown to my room and as I threw my case on the bed the biggest wave of relief washed over me. I was finally going to get the help I needed to stop drinking, I was going to get the opportunity to take some time and figure myself out. I was going to eat three meals a day and get a proper night's sleep for the first time in a long time without passing out from alcohol. I was very happy that I was finally dealing with a problem that had consumed my life.

The doctors immediately put me on the medication Librium, which was fantastic because the paranoia and the DTs didn't really set in. The medication made everything balance out and I didn't experience the horrors. I was just floating around the place for a week. It was a new world for me; it was the first time I had been given the opportunity to have an in-depth look at myself. I began to start having the courage, with professional help, to examine my past and myself as a person and the reasons that made me drink excessively. It was the first time that, as an adult, I had spent any time with myself alone and sober and I took to the programme with every ounce of my being. I spent a lot of time soul-searching, meditating, and reflecting on my life.

With both individual therapy and group therapy, I felt comfortable and supported, and once I started talking I could not stop. The more I spoke the lighter my burden became. I opened up about the abuse I had suffered as a child, which I had never done before. I finally had the strength to face the memories and begin dealing with them. With the self-realisation about why I drank the way I did, I stopped running from the past and began to understand how I could find my way again back to the bubbly, fun-loving person I had been. I needed to rediscover my lust for life, find a new path away from the vicious cycle of needing alcohol to hide from the hurt. I worked hard at healing myself and began on my road to recovery.

It was also the first time I had eaten properly in ten years, a breakfast, lunch and dinner. The food and rejuvenation programme made me feel very well again. I didn't have any cravings for alcohol and I didn't miss my chaotic, booze-fuelled life. Near the end of the programme I was allowed out for the weekend, providing I didn't do anything stupid like have a drink – and I didn't. I could have walked into a pub and ordered my old friend gin and tonic or nipped into an off-licence for a bottle of booze, but I didn't because I liked the new me. There was no temptation for me because I just didn't want to drink any more. I had done so much damage to myself with alcohol that I started seeing it as my enemy. The decision to enter St Pat's was one of the best of my life; I was ready to give it up and I just needed someone to make me take that step. The day I walked out of St Patrick's Hospital I felt positive, strong, determined and ready embrace my new life without alcohol.

9

The Next Step

He who does not reflect his life back to God in gratitude does not know himself.
– Albert Schweitzer

When I came out of rehab the world looked completely different to me. For the first time in my life I was actually seeing things clearly, and it was a relief not to have to pretend to be someone else for a change. I was very happy to be free from the chains of alcohol and I vowed to myself that I would not drink again. I was walking around with a permanent smile on my face. Tackling my alcohol problem was the best thing I ever did and I was overjoyed to be back to myself again. I had my life back and I was in control of it for the first time in years.

I went to AA meetings to ensure I stayed off alcohol. I tried my best to attend the meetings regularly to keep me on the right path, and I managed to go to them consistently for the first year of my sobriety. But at that time in my life I felt they were not right for me; I didn't understand them. I didn't want to be sitting around talking – I wanted to be out living my life. I was enjoying being clean and sober and loved the clarity it gave me. My sense of humour bounced back and it wasn't a hardship for me to stay away from alcohol. I was full of excitement about my future and had boundless energy. I changed my lifestyle completely. Gone were the days of long boozy lunches, nightclubs and people whose social scene revolved around alcohol. I simply didn't go to pubs or hang around with people who did. I avoided any environment where I could be tempted to revert to my old behaviour. I found other things to do rather than putting myself in a position where I would want to drink. I surprised myself, as I never wanted a drop of alcohol or had a craving for it.

I was nervous about starting back at the Four Seasons. I was unsure how people would react to me or what my managers would think of me. I wondered if they would still let me be in charge of the restaurant alone and worried that I might even lose my job. The grand opening of the hotel happened without me and it was up and running for five weeks when I came out of St Pat's. After the big build-up and anticipation surrounding the opening, I had missed it. I am sure a lot of people were under immense pressure but I realised, for the first time, that the world didn't stop when I needed to take some time out. My colleagues and the management were fantastic and very supportive when I returned to the hotel. They welcomed me back and took away any awkwardness I had. A director of the Four Seasons became a really good friend of mine and looked after me. Every Monday night, which was my night off, we went out for dinner to a different restaurant around Dublin. As I had been away from Ireland for so long, I didn't know the new places to eat so we had our dinner date once a week and I enjoyed rediscovering the city with good food and great company. She was not a big drinker, which really helped. She enjoyed a glass of wine with dinner while I had my cranberry juice or water. I found a strength I always knew I had in me, as I was able to cope with seeing other people having a drink, but never longed to have one myself. I spent every day in the hotel serving customers wine and every other alcohol under the sun but I no longer craved it. Also, as I was so busy at work, I didn't have time to even think about drinking, never mind actually doing it. I was free from its hold on me and I loved it.

Being back in a busy restaurant was like a dream come true for me and exactly what I needed. I spent every night running up and down that restaurant, chatting to customers and having a great time. I had a new lease of life. My motivation, drive and ambition returned and my sense of humour, which I had lost in my dark days of drinking, was back in full swing as I happily entertained the clientele of the hotel. I worked very hard; I felt I owed the hotel management something because they had done so much for me, helping me get my life back on track. They had been there for me when I needed help most and I was lucky enough to still have such a great job. I was determined not to let them down.

The restaurant was very expensive and the clientele expected excellent gourmet food and impeccable service. The training for staff was superb and the standards were exceptionally high. However, the service could be a bit stiff, it lacked warmth. It was very much 'Please, sir' and 'Thank you, madam', but there was no sense of fun. I countered this with my enthusiasm, energy and gift of the gab. I had bountiful experience from London at making guests feel welcome and special. I hit the floor in the restaurant and charmed the customers. We love the formalities of fine dining in this country, but we also like to be recognised and to get a bit of banter going with the staff.

It was a truly beautiful hotel and very quickly became the place to be seen. The Four Seasons became a hotspot for celebrities, business people who made money very quickly during the Celtic Tiger, and socialites dressed in over-the-top designer clothes. It was a new world for many of these people, who found themselves very rich in a very short period of time. Having been out of the country for years, I didn't know who was who in this fast-living society. But I made it my business to find out. I did my homework. On my occasional days off I studied all the magazines – *Tatler, VIP, Social and Personal* – and with a marker highlighted the people I had seen in the restaurant. I studied them and found out who they were, who they were married to, who their mistress was, what car they drove, what designers they liked to wear and what hobbies they enjoyed. I already knew a lot of the established wealthy well-respected families but I had to learn about the 'new money' in Dublin society, and I did. I also kept up on what was happening in the courts as judges, barristers and lawyers frequented the restaurant on a regular basis. I ensured I had something to talk about to every customer who stepped into my restaurant, be it the latest trial in the Four Courts or the most recent Gucci catwalk collection.

I couldn't stand any negative TV, such as detective shows or thrillers with violence and murder, so when I got home from work I tried to unwind by watching hours of fashion shows. I watched all the latest shows from New York, Paris and Milan. It was happy TV and it was a great way to learn everything I needed to know about designers, as all my customers wore the latest pieces straight from the catwalk. The minute they stepped into the restaurant I recognised their latest buy; the ladies who lunched and the glamourpusses that came to the Four Seasons loved it when I gushed over their new Gucci or Roberto Cavalli dress. All the socialites wanted to be seen in their expensive designer clothes so I always made sure they were. I wanted to make them visible in the restaurant because they made such an effort to come out looking fabulous. I walked them down the long way to their table, while chatting to them and complementing them on their new outfit and seating them in the middle of the restaurant. I knew who had new diamonds, new dresses and new flash cars. I knew where they went on holidays and who had bought a second or third property. There was great competition among them and I did get a little kick out of winding them up. I enjoyed asking one customer if she had seen another person's fabulous new Armani dress, or the massive diamond ring her husband bought for her while they were on holidays in Monte Carlo.

I had only been running the restaurant in the Four Seasons for a year when I was approached in 2001 to do *The Restaurant* show for RTÉ. the Firm Hotel and Catering Recruitment agency were employed by the broadcaster to visit each of the top hotels and restaurants in Dublin to find a manger that would be suitable for the show. When Kieran Moore from the company first approached me about being part of the show, my initial reaction was 'No way, definitely not'. I did not want to be part of a reality show as I thought it would be a crass way of making fun of me, depicting a camp restaurant manager mincing around screaming his head off.

My mannerisms are very camp; I am vivacious and I admit that, at times, I have been known to be dramatic. I was aware of my characteristics, and I didn't want them to be crudely caricatured on a reality TV show. I had just got my life back together and I didn't want to expose myself on TV to people tuning in for a night's entertainment. I just wanted to get on with my job in the hotel to the best of my ability, so I turned the offer down. But they were not giving up that easily. The concept and style of the show were explained to me and I was assured it was going to be very professional, but I still didn't totally believe them. They managed to convince me to do a screen test and the executives said I was perfect because of my natural ability to talk. I was very animated onscreen, so they tried to convince me to take a chance and take the job, but my answer was still no. Eventually, after a lot of persuading, I did agree to take part in the pilot, which would only be seen by the executives in RTÉ. Sean Moncrieff was the guest celebrity chef for the show, whose aim was to try and impress the food critics with his culinary talents. It was the first time I had ever been in front of TV cameras and I was very nervous. They had to do at least six takes, as I kept getting my lines muddled. The executives liked what they saw. I was offered the role again and Sean was asked to be the narrator. Kieran guaranteed me it was going to be a proper food show and I trusted him so in the end I agreed to be part of *The Restaurant* and I never looked back.

It was very difficult to watch myself on TV; I am my own worst critic. The first time I saw myself on the show I went straight out got my teeth bleached. I also got a spider vein on my forehead removed with laser treatment. And the camera does add ten pounds, I can vouch for

Doing the show really helped me. As soon as I became the restaurant manager on TV, people started recognising me – I was a novelty. My customers knew me and loved talking about the show. The restaurant in the Four Seasons became my stage where I entertained my audience every night. There were constantly celebrities staying in the hotel, but I was never star-struck or flustered by their fame. I knew how to make them feel comfortable and always made sure they got everything they wanted. One such celebrity and his partner stayed in the hotel for a couple of days and on an extremely busy Saturday night, his personal assistant informed me he wanted to dine in the restaurant. The place was packed and I was run off my feet and now I was faced with a very well-known figure strutting into the restaurant. I knew that if he came into the packed restaurant there was going to by mayhem, with customers desperate to meet him and get his autograph. The place was already buzzing and I just knew I had to keep him out of the restaurant, so I suggested to his personal assistant that he would be more comfortable in our private dining room. She went off to him with the proposal and thank God he went for it. I rushed into the private dining room and laid this impressive long table that could sit up to twenty people for him and his partner. I made sure there was wine, red and white, champagne and bottled water. When they arrived I presented him with five different available menus. I left them to decide what they wanted and when I returned to take their order, I found myself standing there in awkward silence for what seemed an eternity as he sat looking at the table. He was very shy and did not say a word. As I stood there my head was racing, thinking about all I needed to do on the floor and I needed to get back into the busy restaurant. In the end I just blurted out, 'How this works is you tell me what you want to eat and drink and I get it for you'. I think he may have been a bit shocked by me speaking so directly to him, but it broke the ice and he just started laughing. Later that night, as service was finishing up, the personal assistant appeared again. It had been a long night and I was exhausted. I was saying a silent prayer he was not looking for something that would be too difficult to provide. He had clearly enjoyed his night as he wanted to know where to go to hear live music in Dublin. As I wasn't drinking and spending practically every waking moment working, I was stumped, but I finally came up with three venues and after the personal assistant vetted them, they went off for a night out. I had filled my obligations and now some other poor soul was going to be confronted with a pop star rocking into their venue and them having to ensure he was not mobbed.

An American rock star and his band, along with his wife and the other musicians' partners, stayed in the hotel when they had a concert in Dublin. They may look like hardcore rock 'n' rollers but they are all gentlemen and enjoy good food and fine wine. When they finished their performances they were most certainly not partying into the early hours of the morning or throwing TVs out of hotel windows. They loved to unwind over a leisurely meal, chatting about the show they had just performed. They all sat around a big table in the middle of the restaurant enjoying their meal and a couple of bottles of nice wine. They were very polite and didn't mind if other customers came over to them for a chat or looking for an autograph.

A Motown legend also stayed in the hotel when she was playing in

Dublin and nobody caught a glimpse of her in the hotel. None of the customers or even the staff saw her even once. The staff only knew she was there because we were told, otherwise we would never have guessed. She arrived into the hotel through the underground car park, in a car with blacked-out windows. She was whisked straight up to the penthouse apartment and remained there until it was time for her to leave for her concert. I was very impressed by how discreet she was.

Gerry Ryan was one of my most well-known, regular customers at lunchtime and I loved to see him coming in as he was always so warm and entertaining. He was the same on the radio as off it; he had time for everybody and was lovely to everyone he met, be it staff or customers. He came into the restaurant most days after his radio show and would be on a high after being on the airwaves, full of banter and funny stories. He sat at the same table every time he came in and usually ordered the same thing to eat. He enjoyed a few glasses of good wine and he adored his whiskey, but he always knew when to stop. He was a very intelligent man and was very comfortable in his own skin. He loved having a good conversation and was able to entertain a whole table over lunch. He loved having a laugh and if someone he knew came into the restaurant there would be good-humoured teasing going on across the room. I always made sure he had a standing reservation for Sunday lunch and he was a regular customer on that day with his family. I had the utmost respect for Gerry Ryan, he was a true gentleman.

The restaurant was my kingdom and it ran it like clockwork. I spent the whole time running around being fabulous and making sure people got what they wanted. Many people wanted the formal dining but some wanted a more casual meal and ate in the café, which didn't take reservations. But everyone wanted to be made a fuss of and that is where I excelled – I knew how to make people feel special. I was flexible and I always made sure my customers got what they wanted; there was no room for error. I made my role indispensable. People wanted to see me and talk to me when they came into the restaurant, so I constantly felt I had to be there, which created a lot of pressure for me, but because I loved my job so much I wanted to be there. I needed to be on the floor for breakfast, lunch and dinner. I went into work at 11 AM and I was still in the restaurant most nights at midnight. I always worked Friday and Saturday night, running both the restaurant and the café. The café seated 38 and I would end up doing 120 covers in there and the restaurant, which seated 80, would do 110.

The kitchen ran five menus consecutively, so it was bedlam at the weekends. Somebody had to be in control and keep it all running smoothly and that was me. The chef was in charge of the kitchen and getting the food out and I was in control of everything else. The triangle between the door, the furthest table in the restaurant and the kitchen was huge. The room was really long and for me to run from the door to the end of the room, to the kitchen and back out again was a lot. I was doing the women's mini-marathon every night. I was walking for miles, while having five different conversations with five different groups of guests. I hit every table twice, talking non-stop.

I also ran the café from memory. I had two hostesses in there and they had to be my right and left hands and know what was going on. I went through a lot of hostesses, if I couldn't trust them to do their job to the standard I expected, then they had to go. Mistakes could not be made as people were paying a lot of money for the service. In the main dining room people were paying up to €100 a head, so we had to deliver good food and good service, complete with compliments, chat and one-liners from me. I had to make everyone feel like they were the most important person in the restaurant.

I was hyper the whole time, my head was constantly racing with what had to be done, but on the outside I was calm and professional. If I needed a staff member's attention on the other side of the room I could do it with one look. I never allowed anyone in a suit who worked in the hotel to walk through my restaurant; they always had to walk around the around the edge of the room because if they walked among the tables, a customer could ask for something and if it was not their table they could forget and there would be complaints, which was just not acceptable. Even if the general manager of the hotel needed to speak to me he stood at the door until I went to him because he knew this was my territory and that he couldn't mess up my system as it ran so smoothly.

The restaurant was very profitable. Sunday mornings were hectic; we served several hundred for breakfast, finished at 11 AM and turned the room in twenty minutes to open for lunch and another busy sitting. And after all that, we had dinner to serve in the restaurant and the Café. The festive season was one of our busiest times and Christmas Day was just insane. During the five days in the run up to Christmas there was breakfast with Santa, the Mad Hatters Tea Party and of course the reservations for Christmas dinner. Christmas dinner in the restaurant was a nightmare as we had a room full of families who may not see each other that much throughout the year sitting around the same table and tension was often high. It was my job to make sure they enjoyed Christmas Day so I spent my time complementing the mothers-in-law on their designer dresses, giving children crayons and colouring books to keep them busy so the frazzled mums could enjoy their meals, and cutting husbands off the wine for a while so they wouldn't get messy.

I was doing all this and they didn't even realise it was happening. I did the same for all my customers. When there were business people in the restaurant with important clients I stayed by them to ensure the people they were entertaining had their wine glasses topped up and everything they needed. If I ensured these things were looked after, then the business people could relax and concentrate on the deals being negotiated.

The table plan could be tricky, as I was constantly trying to avoid awkward encounters between people. It was my job to know who was having affairs, who was getting divorced and which friends had fallen out and make sure they never came face to face in my restaurant. I had to know what was going on among the society crowd to keep everything on the level while they dined. On one occasion there was this high-profile divorce happening between a businessman and his wife. His mother was a notoriously controlling woman and one day she walked into the restaurant and her daughter-in-law's brother was already there having a business lunch. I watched anxiously as she was ushered to a table that would have placed her directly in his line of view. He would have devoured her if he had seen her and there undoubtedly would have been a showdown on the floor. I ran down the restaurant, intercepted the woman and diverted her, telling her there was a much better table for her and explaining the awkward encounter narrowly missed while smiling all the time. She was very grateful I had spotted the potentially disastrous situation and prevented it from happening.

Not only did I look after my customers when they were in my restaurant, I made sure they were given special treatment when they were in other countries on holidays or business trips. I knew a lot of people working in hotels and restaurants all over the world, including in many of my clientele's favourite places such as Italy, America, the south of France, Paris, London and Mauritius. Networking with people in the industry to make sure your customers got looked after was very important and I was a dab hand at it. I was constantly emailing people all over the globe to get my customers' hotel bedrooms upgraded, or to get them a good table in a top restaurant. Once I heard one of my customers was going to a certain country, I got onto my contacts so that the minute they walked to the concierge desk, whether in LA or the Algarve, they were made a fuss of. A female client rang me in a panic one Sunday from New York. She was stranded with no money, credit cards and nowhere to stay as her handbag had been stolen. The first person she thought of ringing to help her was not her family or close friends, but me. I was immediately on the phone fixing it for her and within half an hour, I had her booked into a hotel and had arranged for management there to ensure she got anything she needed and a loan of money. I always looked after my customers and it was a joy for me to do it. Also, when people were visiting Ireland from other countries, I got emails and phone calls from my contacts in hotels and restaurants across the world and I ensured they were looked after here too. My customers were always very appreciative of the lengths I went to to ensure their experience was as good as possible, be it while they were in my restaurant or visiting an international hotel.

At Christmas time my regulars showered me with presents, fabulous gifts which I always really loved getting as it showed they appreciated what I did for them throughout the year. I wanted to please everyone so it was lovely when they recognised that. I always wore nice suits and I had a collection of expensive ties, each one costing hundreds of euro. I bought a designer tie every time I went to visit a city and my regular customers knew that, so I got beautiful Hermes and Armani ties from them as gifts for Christmas.

Four Seasons staff could stay in any other hotel in the chain, anywhere in the world. It was a brilliant opportunity to stay, surrounded by sheer glamour, in some of the most luxurious hotels in the world. But I very rarely felt like I could take time off work and often when I did stay in a Four Seasons hotel abroad, I struggled to shut off my mind and relax as I was constantly watching how they ran the hotel and restaurant. It was like going on holidays in your place of work, which is not conducive to unwinding and recuperating. However, a year after leaving rehab and not drinking, I treated myself to a holiday in Australia for Mardi Gras in Sydney with my best mate Gary and a couple of other friends from London.

Despite all the travelling I had done, I had never been to Australia and I had always wanted to go there for Mardi Gras. It was a present to myself for being sober a year. I took three weeks off work, which was a huge deal for me, and off I went. I had arranged for myself and Gary to stay a couple of nights in the Four Seasons in Sydney, the tickets for one of the biggest parties in the world were in our hands and I was ready to let loose after working so hard for the past twelve months. All the lads couldn't believe I had stayed sober for a year, and that I was planning to party at Mardi Gras without drinking. I didn't touch a drop of booze . . . but I did do a cartload of drugs. I had not touched drugs since leaving London, except for a joint after a long shift at work to help me sleep, but I stupidly thought I could have a blow out on drugs as long as I didn't drink alcohol. My foolish logic was it was alright to take drugs at Mardi Gras, as I was not breaking my commitment to abstaining from alcohol. It was a crazy way to think, but I was able to justify it to myself. I took a mixture of drugs, from ecstasy to cocaine, to get me into the music and keep me going all night. While Mardi Gras was on nobody slept and I wanted to make sure I didn't miss a moment of it. There is nothing bigger on the gay calendar than Mardi Gras in Sydney and now I was there, I was going to party.

But taking drugs had lost its attraction for me, it was not who I was any more. There was a point during one of the nights that Gary found me sitting on my own. I was playing head games with myself and was not in a good place. He told me that if I didn't want to take drugs any more then I shouldn't, but if I was going to take them that weekend to at least enjoy it. I had a ball that weekend but I realised I was finished with that part of my life. I suppose I had to see if I could live that lifestyle just one more time, but I knew it just wasn't for me. I decided I was retiring from the dance floor as I was getting too old and my life had changed, my priorities were different now. That was the end of that chapter in my life and I was delighted I did it that way. After the craziness of Mardi Gras, myself and Gary headed off to Melbourne to spend time with his family and just chill out. The rest of our time in Australia was beautifully relaxing, spent enjoying barbecues with his relatives, sightseeing and going on leisurely trips along the coast.

I had finished the phase of my life that involved taking drugs, but cocaine was rife back in Dublin society . It had become the rich person's drug of choice during the Celtic Tiger and some elements of society had become out of control because of all the money they had made. Suddenly they had all this wealth and they didn't know how to handle it. They lost the run of themselves and were living really over-the-top, extravagant lives. These people were buying yachts, huge mansions, big flash cars, designer clothes, diamonds, holiday homes and building up massive property portfolios in Ireland, and jetting to exotic destinations like South America and the Bahamas.

The money manifested itself into greed. Drinking wasn't enough for them any more, they wanted new highs and cocaine was their answer. They could buy anything their hearts desired without even looking at the price tag so they had to find another way to get their kicks, and cocaine was their vehicle. It was what I call the 'Fendi bag era'. The Fendi bag was the accessory to have in Dublin at the time. A little clutch bag cost €35,000 and all the ladies had to have one. One night as I walked through a crowded bar I spotted this woman in the latest designer dress, manicured nails, a mane of curled extensions and heavy make-up, shovelling cocaine out of her Fendi bag with a little spoon and snorting it in the bar in front of people. For me, that was the epitome of the greed of the Celtic Tiger. It was acceptable to take cocaine within this section of society, so people didn't hide it.

When I gave up alcohol things began to fall into place, it was like a higher power realised I was trying to make my life better and so it gave me what I needed. I bought an apartment in Dublin overlooking the canal with beautiful views of the tranquil water below, which was perfect for calming my mind after a long, gruelling shift in the restaurant. It was my own space that gave me peace from the chaotic outside world.

It was in 2001 I got the phone call from my old school friend from Newbridge College, now living in New York, who had broken the silence as a child about the abuse Fr Vincent Mercer had inflicted on him. He told me he had filed a report with the Director of Public Prosecutions, so the Dean of the Dominican Order now knew all that had happened to us in the 1970s. That phone call was another turning point in my life. The Dean of the Order asked to meet me, so I went along to the Dominican Provincialate headquarters in Tallaght to see him. I opened up and told him the whole story. That one meeting started a whole process of reflection and realisation, which led to a long and winding path of counselling and analysis. I went to a child sex therapist for a year, which was when I really started chipping away at all the pain and hurt I had built up inside. It was a new and terrifying experience to talk about the abuse, but it started me on a journey of healing that I have been on for the last ten years. It was like a key had been put in the ignition and now I was brave enough to pass back through all those dark memories and meet those demons I had locked away for so long. My childhood abuse was suppressed deep within, like a ball of evil energy within me. It had taken me a long time to build it up so it was going to take me a long time to break it down, but at least I had started dealing with it. Fr Mercer was given a three-year suspended sentence for sexually abusing six schoolboys in Newbridge College, as well as two more boys at a holiday camp in Cork.

My road to recovery had begun. I had created a good, positive life for myself in Dublin; I was finally beginning to deal with my abuse as a child, which I had spent my life running from, I had my own home, and I was free from the chains and constrictions of drugs and alcohol. I was surrounded by good, close friends whom I could rely on, *The Restaurant* was a success and the restaurant in the Four Seasons was going from strength to strength with me at the helm. I was making a lot of money and I was doing very well. I didn't need my old life to prove anything to myself because I had this new one.

But there was no way I could continue working at the pace I was, I just didn't know it at the time. I was working ridiculously long hours in a stressful job where I had made my role indispensable. I pushed myself to the brink, refusing to take time off as I had to be in my restaurant to make sure everything was perfect for my bosses and my customers. But trying to achieve perfection in a job every day for seven years is impossible, we are only human. I was not eating right because I just hadn't time, I lived on black coffee, cigarettes and the occasional toasted sandwich, and I couldn't sleep because my head was constantly racing. I was pushing myself to exhaustion constantly and it was only a matter of time until it would all come crashing down around me. And it did.

10

Losing Heart

To strive, to seek, to find and not to yield.
- Tennyson

Work became my new addiction. I made my role as manager in the restaurant indispensable and created a gruelling schedule for myself, often working long hours, six days a week. I felt like I had to be there the whole time to ensure my customers' dining experience was flawless. I thought I was doing extremely well, as I was not drinking and I wanted to put everything into my job. I had the restaurant running like clock-work and when I was not there, things tended to go wrong. I made myself the face of the restaurant and with that came a lot of pressure. I was on the floor of the restaurant for breakfast, lunch and dinner because I believed I had to be there. I started work at 10.30 AM and kept going non-stop until midnight. I was doing double shifts, day in day out, six days a week. I never took a weekend off as I would feel ashamed if my regular customers came in and I wasn't there to welcome them and entertain them. I would have felt too guilty if I wasn't there making sure the restaurant was running smoothly.

My work ethic had become increasingly more relentless over the years. It started to take a toll on me, but I didn't see it at the time. Other managers warned me that I was too consumed by my job and I was doing too much but I didn't listen to them. I loved what I was doing and I kept pushing myself to excel at it.

I lived on cigarettes and coffee. I was too busy to smoke much while I was at work, but when I went home I chain-smoked up to twenty cigarettes, one after the other. I was constantly drinking coffee, starting with a double espresso in the morning and after that there was always a strong cup of coffee at the food pass; which I kept topped up throughout the whole day and night; sipping at it every chance I got. I pumped myself full of caffeine. I had litres of coffee and sparkling water every day and very little food. I couldn't work on a full stomach as it sapped my energy, slowing me down, so I always just had something light to eat. The hotel staff had their dinner at 5 PM and the food provided for us was excellent. Every day there was a choice of two main courses, a vegetarian option and a full salad bar. But I never opted for a full meal. Despite there being an array of mouth-watering dishes on offer, I usually just had a toasted sandwich, which I would hardly ever finish. After work, when my adrenalin levels dropped, I was always starving but I just couldn't face a lot of food after smelling it and looking at it for hours. I was also always too tired to face eating so I just grabbed a bowl of chips or another toasted sandwich. My diet was atrocious but I was too busy to worry about it.

Hyper and highly strung when my shift ended, I really struggled to sleep. I just couldn't switch off my mind and relax. I sat in my apartment running over things that happened that night at work and planning what I had to do the next day. If it had been a particularly hectic shift, I would still be awake at 4 AM, despite having to get up for the breakfast service the next day. Gin and tonics, vodka and wine use to help me unwind and I would pass out, but now I didn't have them. As I was so exhausted and needed to sleep, I started using cannabis. I smoked a joint most nights to help me fall asleep. I thought that once I wasn't drinking, it was fine. On my rare days off I just slept and ate. I had no social life, as the last place I wanted to go was a crowded bar or nightclub. Even during my free time I couldn't stop thinking about work; fretting about if everything was running alright in the restaurant without me and worrying about what I had to do when I went back to work.

Christmas in the Four Seasons left me very stressed but I always worked right through the festive season, including Christmas Day. However, come St Stephen's Day I was off and regularly took three weeks' holidays to unwind and recuperate. But in 2007 the assistant manager wanted time off in January so I had to continue working right through. I was in over-drive and exhausted but I had to keep going. I thought the restaurant would have been quiet after Christmas but it remained extremely busy. Friends and families who had not had time to catch up over the festive season were meeting for dinner, and of course the socialites that had been away skiing were eager to have dinner with their friends and tell them about their fabulous holidays.

The pressure was really getting to me and I could feel the strain of my work schedule but I was so use to being a pivotal part of the restaurant that I just kept going. I had a Tuesday and Wednesday off in

January to film *The Restaurant* in Athlone and I was exhausted. On the Wednesday night after we had finished recording, I calmly turned to Elaine Normile, who was on the show and also my flatmate and my friend, and told her I was going to have a couple of glasses of wine. She looked completely shocked and dumbfounded that I was going to break my sobriety. I told her she was not to freak out and make an issue about it. Seven years without a drink and I didn't even think twice about opening that bottle of red wine, pouring myself a glass and drinking it.

I didn't plan it, it just happened and I had no big moral debate in my head about whether I should or not. I hadn't been attending AA meetings and thought I would cope fine with having a couple of glasses of wine and that it would be no big deal. How wrong I was. I got very drunk that night. I didn't feel any guilt about it though, I justified it to myself that I was working so hard and I was stressed and needed to unwind. I felt I deserved a drink, so I had a lot of them. I had a terrible hangover the next day and driving home I was as sick as a dog. I spent the day on the sofa eating junk food and then went back to work on Thursday.

While on the floor in the restaurant I felt this very strange sensation; like my heart had skipped a beat or had jumped. It was like my heart had stopped and started again. My face drained of colour and my lips went blue. One of my colleagues saw me and was extremely concerned but of course I told him I was fine, and kept working. I just put it down to the stress of the job. I ran around the restaurant chatting to customers until 10 PM when one of the hostesses took me aside and told me I looked like hell and I needed to go home. I eventually admitted I didn't feel well and went back to my apartment.

When I got home I sat down on my armchair with a cup of tea and a cigarette. I watched TV with Elaine until midnight and finally decided I was tired enough to go to bed. As I lay there in the dark I felt agitated and really short of breath. There was no tightness in my chest; I just couldn't catch my breath. I opened the window behind the headboard of my bed to try and get some air. When I stood up the blood drained from my face like sand in an egg timer and I knew that I was in trouble. I didn't have a pain in my chest but it was beginning to feel uncomfortable. I came out to the living room and sat on the sofa. Elaine was still up and asked me if I was alright and I was still saying I was fine. But then I got a pain in my arm and I realised I could be having a heart attack.

I always imagined that a person having a heart attack would collapse to the floor in agony, clutching their chest. It was not as dramatic as that, but I knew the symptoms I was experiencing were those of a heart attack. I calmly told Elaine to ring an ambulance as I needed to go to the hospital, still telling her I was fine. I was having heart attack and I was still trying to convince someone I was alright! I remember looking at the clock and it was 1 AM, then I must have lost consciousness because when I looked at it again it was 1.07 AM and there were two paramedics standing over me. Two gorgeous men, I wasn't sure if I was still alive or if I had died and gone to heaven.

I told them I was having pains in my chest and down my arm and I wasn't feeling very well. I explained I had just finished work; I had been very busy over Christmas and I was stressed. They were looking around the apartment and I knew they were examining the place to see if there was alcohol or drugs. I told them I had not been drinking or taking any drugs. They informed me they were going to take me to the ambulance to check my heart with the ECG machine, but I was going nowhere in the tracksuit bottoms and shabby T-shirt I was wearing. I strolled into my bedroom and changed into jeans, a shirt and jumper and grabbed my coat. When I came back into the living room the two paramedics and Elaine were looking at me like I was a mad man. I was having a heart attack but I still had to look presentable.

One of the paramedics asked me did I want him to carry me to the ambulance, and in normal circumstances I would have been more than happy to be in his arms, but I told him I could walk. It was a really stormy night with strong winds. As I lay down, the ambulance was being shaken by the wind and I could hear it howling. One of the paramedics hooked me up to the ECG and within seconds he was banging on the window for the other paramedic to drive; the doors of the ambulance were slammed and they sped to the hospital. It was at that moment I let go and I began to feel myself losing consciousness.

I was in St Vincent's Hospital within minutes and the doctors had my jumper off, shirt open and were using crash pads on me almost immediately. They took blood tests and twenty minutes later a nurse came to me and confirmed I was having a heart attack and that it was quite serious. I lay on the trolley in a cubicle on my own at 3 AM trying to digest the news. I was frightened. But for some strange reason I knew I was not going to die, that I was going to get through it and be fine. I was in pain, but it was not unbearable and I drifted in and out of sleep.

At 7.30 AM the CAT lab where they do angiograms was opened and I was wheeled up in my trolley to be seen by cardiologist, Martin Quinn.

A line was put through my groin and I was shown an X-ray of my heart by the doctor. Modern technology is a wonderful, fascinating thing; I was able to see clearly the blockage in one of my arteries. Because of the medication I was on it was quite surreal and didn't bother me, I just thought it was phenomenal. The nurses were so caring the way they spoke to me; reassuring me all the time that I was going to be alright, and I believed them. Dr Quinn explained what he was doing the whole time. I didn't panic as I knew I was in the right place to get the help I needed and in very safe hands. When the doctor put the stent in the pain just stopped. It was amazing. I was brought to CCU and put on a monitor; I felt like I was in a scene from *ER*. A few hours ago I was on the restaurant floor and now I was lying in hospital after having a heart attack.

Lying in my bed back in the ward a wave of relief came over me as I realised I was going to have to take time off work. I was not able to do my job; I was being given time away from my responsibilities guilt free. It was like being handed a get out of jail free card. Time to sleep, rest and eat in the hospital and it wasn't my fault that I couldn't go to work. I was delighted. I stayed in my hospital bed for ten days. I didn't care about what was happening in the restaurant and it was such a relief to be allowed to feel like that. The only thing I had to concentrate on was my health. The management in the hotel were great and told me everything was fine and the main priority was to get well.

My family came to visit me and it was difficult for them to see me lying in a hospital bed after having a heart attack, knowing I could have died. When my mother came into the ward and saw me, she broke down in tears. She was very upset. I am her only son and the thought that she could have lost one of her children was a lot for her to take in. She sat beside my bed and we talked for a long time. She was very emotional but I reassured her that everything was going to be fine and I had got through it and was going to come out the other side.

The medics had explained to me what had happened; why I had a heart attack so young. I was told there was a partial blockage in another artery and that I was going to have to start looking after my health better. After a couple of days, I was taken off the morphine. I got out of bed and sat on a chair beside my hospital bed. Looking out the window at the blue sky, the tears started flowing. Once they started I couldn't stop crying. It was like the flood gates had opened and all the emotions inside me came gushing out. A nurse came over to see if I was alright. I told her I had done enough drugs in my day to know my emotions were due to coming off the morphine; it was like a come-down after a weekend of partying. But this time I knew it was different; it was more than just coming down of the morphine. It was the first time I realised I was not invincible.

While in hospital, I was inundated with cards, presents and flowers from my customers, friends and family. It was overwhelming and very touching to know how much people thought of me. Trolleys of gifts were wheeled into my ward every day. I sent them all home to my apartment. The place was covered with bunches of flowers and cards with heartfelt messages. The TV company for *The Restaurant* sent me a massive basket of fruit that would have fed a small town in Tipperary for a week. The support and well-wishes meant so much to me.

After ten days I left the hospital and disappeared to my parents' house in Naas. It was so comforting to be back in my old childhood bedroom, where I felt safe and protected. My mother cooked meals for me and looked after me, nursing me back to health. It was such a relief to be away from Dublin and my life of stress. My father gave me breakfast in bed every morning. It was lovely to wake up to my father standing there with a bowl of porridge and toast on a tray for me. Every evening my mother cooked my favourite meals. They cared for me like I was a child again. I gradually began to get my strength back and was able to get up for a couple of hours and go for short walks. For the first time in my life I kept my mobile phone turned off, which was liberating. That thing was usually constantly ringing and attached to my ear. Dealing with phone calls and texts is exhausting, so I didn't do it. I took time out of my life and looked after myself for a change.

I went back to Dublin at the beginning of March. I felt better and was getting restless. I wanted to be back in the city and in my own apartment. I had started missing my life there and felt ready to re-enter it. But it felt strange to be back. It was the same but very different. I felt like my old life was over and I was beginning something new; but I didn't know what that was going to be. All my friends were delighted that I was back on my feet and looking so well. Maria Collins from Rostrover is my closest friend in Dublin and she was there for me so much after my heart attack.

We met at a mutual friend's party in 2001 and ended up sitting beside each other. We chatted and laughed all night long and have been laughing ever since. I can't even remember who else was at that party; we were so engrossed in conversation. Maria is a strong character with outstanding beauty. We became inseparable. We went to functions, lunches, dinners and holidays together and are great supports for each other. She is fabulous company to be with and she is always positive and high energy. She was the perfect person to be around as I tried to build a new life for myself. We went for long lunches together and chatted for hours about what I had been through and what I should do next. I spent time catching up with my friends, meeting them for coffee or something to eat. They all wanted to meet me to make sure I was alright. I was very cautious about what I did as I didn't really know what was good for me and what was bad. I felt great, which was very strange considering I had just had a heart attack. I was constantly going into hospital for tests and was being very careful to look after myself. But I started to drink again occasionally. It was the odd glass of wine with dinner or at the end of the day. My thinking was, I was alive and enjoying a couple of drinks was fine.

Once I had caught up with all my friends I started to get a bit bored. I was used to being busy so I decided to go back to work part-time. I discussed it with the management of the Four Seasons and they agreed that I could work a couple of days a week. It was strange being back in the restaurant. It was very comforting to be there as I felt secure and knew what my role was. The assistant managers ran the place while I was away and did a great job in my absence. They were my people and I was delighted to be working beside them again. But it was difficult to manage the restaurant when I was not there full-time and I struggled to get back into it. The customers were delighted to see me back on the floor and I spent most of the time talking to them. Everyone wanted to know how I was doing.

In June I went on holidays with my mother to Mijas in Spain. I wanted to spend some time in the sunshine relaxing and my mother was the perfect companion to do that with. Maria was in Marbella at the time and I went to visit her. I drank a lot on that holiday and was drunk most nights. Maria and my mother became worried about me while I was there. They voiced their concerns but I didn't want to listen. I was alive and I wanted to live my life and that involved alcohol. They had both started to notice that my behaviour had become erratic and I was acting strangely. I was showing signs of depression. I didn't realise it at the time, but the people closest to me could see what was happening.

When I got home my drinking got heavier. It was my only means of escaping the feeling of hollowness and emptiness I was experiencing. The only time I felt truly alive was when I was drunk. Gin and tonics and bottles of wine became my best friends again. I was constantly anxious and stressed. I was struggling to get out of bed and I had very little motivation. I felt like there was a big dark cloud hanging over me and everything was grey and empty. The euphoria I had experienced post-heart attack was gone. I was suffering from post-traumatic stress (which of course I didn't know at the time) and my excessive drinking was making it worse. I was like a trapped, terrified animal that was scared of my own shadow. I was surrounded by caring people who loved me but I felt alone. I was lost and I had no direction and the darkness was relentless.

In August my world really began to close in on me. It took me longer and longer to get out of the house in the morning to get to work because of the anxiety. Every morning I struggled to get out of my bed; I was frozen with fear, in a knot of anxiety. I couldn't cope with life. At work I constantly had a napkin in my hand to wipe my brow as I was sweating profusely. I was on edge. I was fighting the dark thoughts in my head all the time. The only place I felt safe was in my apartment with a bottle of wine. It became my own little shell, where I could hide from the world and from myself. I was trapped in vicious circle of destruction and depression and it progressively got worse. During the RDS Dublin Horse Show week the hotel was extremely busy and I was stressed. I was constantly putting on a performance, pretending to the outside world I was fine while inside I was falling apart. I always had a smile on my face and a witty comment to make my customers laugh, but it was all pretence and it was exhausting.

One night, as I stood in the middle of the restaurant, which was packed to capacity, a sensation like an electric pulse shot through my spine and into my head. I felt like my head was going to explode. I was terrified, I didn't know what was going on – I thought I was going to die or that I was losing my mind. I walked out of the restaurant and told the general manager I didn't feel right. I told him I didn't know what was wrong with me. I am sure he knew I was suffering from depression, and told me to go to the doctor and take some time off work. But I didn't go to the doctor, as I thought I could work through it myself.

Instead I went to Thailand with Gary and my other friend Thomas, who I knew from London, and it was a disaster. I acted so strangely on that holiday that I am still apologising to them for it to this day. We stayed in the Four Seasons Hotel, which is the most beautiful place to stay in Koh Samui, but I was in hell. It rained the whole time and I just didn't want to do anything. I was an insomniac so I was awake all night drinking and smoking cigarettes and then I couldn't get out of bed during the day. The two boys didn't know what do with me; they were very concerned about me as I was so far from my normal bubbly fun-loving self. All I wanted was to be drunk. I couldn't live in my own head; I just wanted to be numb. As the tropical storms raged outside I spent most of the time drunk in my bedroom watching movies. It may be a paradise island but it didn't matter; I was so blinded by depression that I couldn't see beauty anywhere.

When I got back to Ireland I continued working part-time and pretending to everyone I was fine. But I was not coping, every day was a struggle. I was suffering, but I still refused to ask anybody for help. A doctor, who was a regular customer in the restaurant, recognised I was suffering from depression, and told me so. She wrote a prescription for me but I didn't believe her. I kept the prescription but I never used it. I just got up every morning and put on my suit, which became my armour to protect me from the world. As I had done before, I adopted a false personality. I was very good at pretending, it was my coping mechanism, but it wasn't working. Just after Christmas I went to a friend's house for dinner and as soon as I walked in the door, she knew exactly what was going on with me because she had experience of depression in her family. She sat me down and told me what was happening and told me she was going to take me to a doctor on Monday, and she did. He wrote me a prescription for anti-depressants, the same as the one the doctor in the hotel had prescribed weeks previously. But this time I took them.

Three weeks after I started taking the medication, it started to work. The dark cloud I had been living under dissipated and the sun came out again. Driving to Galway soon after to visit friends, I cried the whole way out of sheer relief. The darkness that had consumed me was gone and I could see the countryside and the beauty around me again. But I was still drinking heavily, even while taking the anti-depressants. I was still hiding from those demons from my childhood by downing alcohol; booze kept them quiet and shut them out of my life. The hotel management had been hugely helpful and understanding after the heart attack, giving me a whole year to recover. But it had come to the point where I had to step up and make work my priority again. I had to start being that charismatic manager once more, to take charge of the restaurant again.

As I was working part-time I was in and out of the restaurant and not fully committed to my job, which was becoming blatantly obvious to my bosses. I wasn't well and I felt like the hotel was closing in on me.

I decided the only way I could feel better was to break free from it and get some space, so I resigned. It was a crazy thing to do but at the time I thought it was my only option. I shouldn't have resigned, I should have just taken a year's sabbatical and used that time to finally confront the child abuse I had suffered; to face my depression and my alcohol addiction. But I just couldn't keep doing it any more; I couldn't keep going into work with a smile plastered on my face and pretend I was alright. My life was crumbling around me and I was panicking. The general manager was new and didn't know me that well. He didn't know how good I was at my job before I had the heart attack and just knew me as the restaurant manager that didn't work a full week, so he let me resign and walk out of the hotel.

As soon as I left the restaurant, I felt like I was free falling down a cliff and there was nobody at the bottom to catch me. Work had been my anchor, the only thing that was consistent, and now it was gone. It was like the rug had been pulled out from under me and I didn't know what to do. I spiralled out of control within a week. All I could rely on was alcohol and cigarettes. I woke up every morning with a hangover and by the afternoon I needed a drink to calm me down, so I opened my first bottle of wine. I was drinking a lot of alcohol on top of my anti-depressants. I also started taking Valium and Xanex – anything I could get my hands on – to help me get away from my life and my thoughts.

Before resigning from the hotel I had started doing some consultancy work with a man called Conor Kenny. We often had to drive across the country at 6 AM to be in Galway or Kerry by 9 AM to run a course. I was often late meeting him, as well as hungover a lot of the time. Thankfully he was a very understanding guy and very in tune with the trials and tribulations of life, and knew I was struggling. I could call him and say I couldn't work that day, as it was often a struggle for me to just leave my apartment. One day we were due to do a course and I simply didn't turn up and didn't call him. I switched my phone off and I went into this black hole. I had been drinking heavily the night before and I was not fit to do what I was meant to do. I was ashamed and frustrated that I had become this person, but the only way I knew how to stop feeling like that was to have a drink. I sat, downing booze in the dark. I believed I would never be able to find my way back to a life full of light and laughter again. I was suicidal. I was not just thinking about killing myself; I was at the stage of planning it. I sat for hours on my own seriously contemplating what method was the best way to kill myself. I visualised my own death; it was a dangerous place to be and I knew I was in serious trouble.

That day I decided I needed help. I rang my mother and asked her for the phone number of the Rutland Centre, as she still had it from the last time my alcoholism had taken hold of my life. This time nobody had to back me into a corner and convince me I needed help; I knew myself that if I didn't tackle my drink problem, I was going to die.

I rang the Rutland Centre that day; it was a Thursday and when they asked me if I could stop drinking I told them I could because I had done it before. I decided that day was going to be the last time I drank and they gave me an appointment for an assessment for the Monday. I wanted to mark the day that I was quitting drinking so I decided to get very drunk on every drop I had in the apartment. The crazy thought process of an alcoholic. I downed every drop of gin and wine in the place and finally, I pulled out a bottle of Cristal from under my bed that I had been given as a Christmas present the year before. I had been saving it for a special occasion. I drank it warm.

Once I had drank all the alcohol in my house I went to sleep. The next morning I went home to my parents' house, had one of my mother's home-cooked dinners, and got into bed and stayed there for three days until it was time to go to rehab. My head was a mess and I was so depressed and full of anxiety; the only place I felt safe was in bed in my childhood room. On Monday morning my sister Mary drove me to the Rutland Centre for my assessment and I was admitted on the Wednesday.

I arrived at the Rutland after being sober for three days. The first thing they did was to take me off all mood-altering medication, including the anti-depressants. When I walked into my bedroom in the centre there was a guy wearing a black vest with both arms covered in tattoos sitting reading the Bible. He was going to be my roommate for the duration of my stay and I panicked. I thought this man is either going to kill me in my sleep, steal from me or rape me. But we ended up becoming soul mates in there. We carried each other through our journeys. You need a friend who understands you when you are going through something like that. We were in the same therapy group and we shared a room, so we became very close. He became my friend for life. After two weeks I was completely dried out and all the madness in my head had stopped. I swore to myself in the Rutland that I would never drink again. I went in there with the attitude that I am going to fix this; I am going to use whatever is given to me to rectify whatever has gone wrong. I was determined to give it my best shot and I didn't care what it was going to take. I was not going to go through this again. Whatever was causing my alcoholism I was going to face it and deal with it head on.

I immersed myself in the programme, which included intensive group therapy twice a day with two very good counsellors. The focus on self-discovery and spirituality was a phenomenal experience for me. Despite time spent previously in rehab and counselling, that was the first time I truly realised how damaged I was and what had been fuelling the alcoholism. It was all going back to the abuse. Any good psychologist could have told me that, and had tried, but I had to discover it for myself. I had to understand my approach to alcohol, to work and my addictive tendencies towards both. I learnt a lot about addiction and how it manifests itself. I did a lot of mediation and Reiki as part of a holistic programme, which I adored. It gave me a chance to really relax and get in touch with myself. My friends and family came to see me and they couldn't believe how I was living. I was not allowed newspapers, mobile phones or television. I was cut off from the outside world to focus on myself and my recovery, and I loved it. I was open to any change that was coming my way. I participated in all the support groups including those for narcotics and alcohol addiction. I did them all because I needed to find myself and discover where I fitted. It was tough, but it really worked for me. I had begun to piece my life back together and I was so relieved to be on the right path. The only bad habit I still had was smoking. While I was in the Rutland, I smoked so much because of all the emotional issues I was dealing with. But I had got a handle on everything else.

I left the Rutland Centre after five weeks on 14 July. I was emotionally drained; very vulnerable and exposed. I had opened up myself and my soul. The only thing I knew to do was go to AA meetings on a daily basis and sit there and listen. I couldn't do anything else. It was the second time I had to find a new life for myself and discover where I fitted in it. It was like being reborn. I had to learn how to live without alcohol. My roommate from the Rutland Centre lived close to me and we helped each other through the next part of our journey. The guys who were in rehab with me became very close friends. We were constantly on the phone to each other and hanging out together. We understood what the other was going through; we went to AA meetings together and became a support system for each other. I told my mother I was going to do whatever it took to get my life back together and I was not going to drink again. I haven't drunk alcohol since and I don't want to, but it took a long time to get to this place. Weddings and funerals are the hardest things to endure, the combination of family and alcohol is never easy to navigate. At the beginning I had to be prepared going to a social event, ensuring I had a way to get out of the situation immediately if I needed to. I always made sure my car was outside so that I could leave straight away if I felt myself getting weak and craving a drink.

In the initial period after leaving rehab I was very careful. I did what my counsellors told me to do and went back every Saturday to the Rutland to check in with them for my aftercare meetings. I did that for a year. The Rutland did so much for me, but I knew I had to do the rest. When I knew I could go no further with the aftercare programme, I left. I was still doing my consultancy work and I was teaching restaurant service in the Galway-Mayo Institute of Technology. I drove to Galway every Thursday, gave classes, stayed with a friend there that night and taught another class on Friday morning before driving back to Dublin. I was making enough money to survive and my life was beginning to come together. I was feeling strong and positive about my future.

In November 2009 I had my eighteen-month sobriety and I was due to go to the Rutland Centre to get my medallion. I was so proud of the progress I had made and I was really looking forward to receiving my medallion. It was recognition of all the hard work I had done to get sober and stay that way. It was a Sunday morning. I was sitting in my armchair with a cigarette in one hand and a mug of coffee in the other, and I had another heart attack.

I couldn't believe it. I was the fittest I had ever been, I was at the gym regularly and had lost 20 kilos, I was running five kilometres three times a week, I wasn't drinking, I wasn't taking drugs, I wasn't stressed at work and I was still having another heart attack. The last thing I had to do was give up the cigarettes and I had decided I was going to quit them after Christmas. My cardiologist Dr Quinn had warned me I had to stop smoking because I had a 50 percent chance of having another heart attack if I didn't. And now it was happening.

When I realised what was happening to me I got into bed and for a split second I thought about not ringing anyone for help. I thought I could not face going through the depression and the anxiety again. I had my mobile in my hand and I just stared at it. I seriously considered not using it and just lying there and dying. But then the faces of my family and friends and all the people I loved flashed into my mind. I rang my neighbour Cliona and told her she needed to come down to me immediately. I was in a lot more pain than the last time, it was excruciating. I clutched my chest and cried out loud in distress. I crawled out of bed, opened the door of my apartment and told Cliona to call an ambulance immediately. I went to my medication bag and got the GTN spray, which helps to open all the blood vessels around the heart. I managed to walk out to the ambulance and told the paramedics I was having my second heart attack. I knew it was serious this time. I thought, This could be it, I am going to die.

When I arrived at St Vincent's Hospital I was lucky that Professor Ken McDonald was doing his rounds. He came straight down to A&E. I was writhing in pain. The minute he saw me he said the operating theatre had to be opened immediately. He carried out a balloon angioplasty, which kept my stents from collapsing. When I gained consciousness after surgery I was very sick. I was slipping into a space where I felt like I was somewhere between life and death and I could go either way. Suspended somewhere between consciousness and unconsciousness, I felt very weak. I called out to whatever is around us, be it spirituality, an energy force, or God to come and help me and I felt I got an answer. I handed over my life to a higher power and let go. I felt this surge of a bright white light illuminate the room and this sense of protection and relief washed over me. I knew I was going to survive. At that moment I knew everything was going to be OK and no harm was going to come to me. I slept very peacefully that night.

Two weeks later they took the balloon out. It was the worst pain I have ever experienced. I left hospital very weak and vulnerable. I knew I had caused the heart attack myself; I shouldn't have been smoking and I knew that. It was at that point I knew I had to take responsibility for my illness and my medication and start looking after myself, my heart and my life. I knew if I didn't do that my life was going to end. I went back to my parents' house again; my safe haven that I returned to every time I needed help and somewhere to feel safe. It was like returning to the womb. It is where I always went to recuperate and find the strength to build myself and my life up again. I lay in my old bed, in my old room and I saw my life like a film play out in front of me. I saw my abusers, who took the trust and innocence of a child and crushed it; my hedonistic days of partying; my family, the charismatic manager who performed in his restaurant; the broken alcoholic, and the survivor of two heart attacks. It was like watching a movie of my life as my memories reset themselves after the trauma of the heart attack. I stayed in the family home for the whole of November.

When I returned to Dublin I just concentrated on eating healthily and building myself back up again. I was freezing all the time. After the heart attack, I just couldn't get warm. I craved to feel the sun on my face and get some heat in my bones. And then, like a gift from God, I was handed the opportunity of a job in Portugal. I was doing MC at a charity auction in the Rutland Centre and a man – who also attended a programme there – was in the audience. He recognised me from *The Restaurant* show and liked my banter and the way I communicated with people. After the auction he approached me and asked if I would be interested in working with him on a project in Portugal. He had turned his beautiful five-bedroom villa, in an enchanting bohemian village in the mountains called Caldas de Monchique in the Algarve, into a guesthouse for recovering alcoholics. He wanted me to open it and run it. It was called Sober Holidays and it was a place were recovering alcoholics could have some time out and relax. Holidays can be a nightmare for recovering alcoholics because so many destinations revolve around bars and booze. The first thing most people do when they get on a plane is order a drink, and when you arrive it can be just about pubs, cocktails and nightclubs. He was offering people a holiday where they could unwind without being surrounded by the temptation of alcohol and drunk tourists falling out of bars.

I jumped at the opportunity; it was perfect for me. There would be sunshine and I could live in a spiritual retreat surrounded by others who were dealing with alcoholism and themselves. I would have time to rediscover myself and gain strength and inner peace. I was not well enough to drive myself, so my roommate from rehab drove me there in my jeep. We drove to Cork, got the ferry to France and drove all the way down through France and north Spain and finally into Portugal. When we arrived I found myself in the most beautiful, serene setting. I fell in love with the place immediately. Somebody had handed me the perfect place to be at that point in my life.

I worked very hard, it kept me busy and I loved it. I picked the guests up from the airport and brought them to the villa. I made breakfast for them in the morning and cooked dinner every evening. I advised them on where to go sightseeing and nearly every day I drove them to the beach. I ensured everybody felt welcome and comfortable in the guesthouse. In the evenings, we had long leisurely meals and shared our stories. Talking about our experiences with other people who had been through similar things gave us strength. Strong bonds and lasting friendships were made in that villa. I also had time to concentrate on myself and spent a lot of time meditating and reflecting on my life.

I stayed in Portugal for nearly a year and enjoyed every minute of it. I returned to Ireland regularly, to attend hospital appointments, and then I was told the news I had secretly been expecting: I needed a heart transplant.

11

Getting on the List

The spirit of a man will sustain him in sickness
— Proverbs 18:14

When my heart failure cardiologist, Dr Rory O Hanlon, told me I needed to have an assessment for a heart transplant, I was not shocked. We had discussed the possibility the previous year and he had said then that I should think about going on the national heart transplant list. I never knew such a thing existed. After my second heart attack, I had had a year in the beautiful, tranquil setting of Portugal to come to terms with the prospect of having to get a heart transplant to survive. I spent a lot of time on my own, sitting, digesting the idea and talking about it with people I had become close to at the villa. I meditated, did Reiki and went on a spiritual journey of self-discovery, so I was in a good place.

Living in the sunshine was very positive for me physically, psychologically and spiritually. I felt strong enough to deal with what had to be done for me to stay alive. I was very accepting of everything that life had given to me and everything I still had to get through. My close friends in Portugal were mostly from the AA meetings and were a great support to me. They had many years of sobriety experience and they had a firm grasp of the spiritual side of the AA program. It was amazing for me to be around them as I learnt so much from their presence and life experience. My time with them played a huge roll in preparing me for what was to come next.

It was the end of the tourist season in Portugal in November and the villa was not busy. I was due to be back in Ireland to record *The Restaurant* and I also needed to return for an assessment for the heart transplant list. It was like everything was working out as it should. It was the natural time to leave Portugal and was coinciding with the other things I had to do in my life back in Ireland. It felt like it was meant to be. I flew home to face my next big challenge of getting on the heart transplant list and waiting for a donor. Everyone was very impressed by my healthy, tanned glow. I looked and felt amazing and was full of the joys of life after my precious time in Portugal, where I had a chance to really be comfortable with myself. I did not look like someone whose heart was going to fail. The doctors in the Mater Hospital needed to see if I was eligible for a transplant and if I would be able to physically survive such a massive operation. I travelled to the Wineport Lodge in Athlone to record the show and on 14 November, I checked into the Mater for a transplant work-up.

I underwent test after test, the doctors must have used every machine in the hospital; nothing went unexamined. The team did MRI scans, bone density tests, blood tests, chest X-rays, tests on my liver, kidneys, colon, gums and even X-rays of my teeth. The tests were unbelievably thorough. The medics had to make sure that if I got the transplant I was infection- and bacteria-free. Everything was in working order, apart from my heart, which was deteriorating at a significant rate and the wall muscles were in a degenerative state.

I was in the hospital for two weeks. My days were spent looking out the window of my ward on the seventh floor of the hospital as heavy snow fell. It snowed for days and everything was covered in a blanket of white. It was a very calming, mystical sight. It also brought the country to a standstill, which meant my family and friends couldn't travel to the hospital to visit me as the roads were too dangerous. I had a lot of time on my own to contemplate what lay ahead of me and the massive challenges I was going to be confronted with. It gave me space to contemplate what the future could hold: the prospect of a long wait for a donor while my heart continued to get weaker; the thought of not getting a heart transplant in time to save me; and the major surgery I would have to undergo to keep me alive if a donor heart did become available. They were life or death scenarios I had to try to come to terms with.

It was important to have a chance to contemplate the idea of getting a new heart and the possibility of not getting one, which were both very overwhelming concepts to face. I had an inner strength and belief that I could face and overcome the challenges that lay ahead. Mentally I felt strong, but physically I was cold all the time. I was so accustomed to the heat from the sun on my skin that the cold really affected me. I was in a building constructed in the 1970s and the windows were single-glazed. The room was north facing, the wind was relentless, the temperature had dropped below zero and the room I was staying in was cold and draughty. When it was finally safe enough for my parents to drive from Naas to the hospital, my mother brought me up my duvet from home. It gave me such warmth and comfort. I wrapped myself up in it and felt much more content.

I was affiliated to one of the transplant coordinators called Zeta Lawler, who was amazing throughout my whole journey. She explained the pre- and post-transplant process to me in great detail. I also met the psychologists, the physiotherapist, the dietician, the pharmacist, the post-transplant nurse, and the pre-transplant nurse. They all came to me one by one and told me what I was going to go through and what their role was going to be. The process was explained to me in great detail a couple of times, so I was under no illusions about what lay ahead. I believe the experts were aware that I was strong enough to handle it and wanted to ensure I knew what I was facing. It was all very informative, open and kind of exciting – I now had the hope of getting a healthy donor heart.

The Restaurant was on TV over Christmas. It was around that time that the story broke in the newspapers that I was on the transplant list. I started doing interviews with journalists and went on radio shows to talk about what I was going through. I didn't realise it at the time, but I was distracting myself from the constant waiting for that call to say there was a donor heart. In each interview I did I opened up a little bit more about my life and what I was going through. I spoke about what had happened in my past that I believed had brought me to the place I found myself in now.

I believe my heart condition was, to some extent, caused by my lifestyle. But I also believe there was a psychological and emotional side that caused it too that I never fully faced. I worked hard and played hard for years, but I don't believe I did more than the man standing beside me in a nightclub or the person working next to me in a restaurant. Why did I have not one, but two heart attacks, and they didn't? What led me to drink so much, take drugs, work to the point of exhaustion and party so hard? I wanted to explain to myself and the little boy inside me what had actually happened, and to make sense of it emotionally.

As I waited for the transplant I used the time to explore my past and try to understand why I was on this life path. I was not strong enough to work and I had limited energy, but I couldn't just sit around doing nothing. I started writing this book, as well as making a documentary about my time waiting for a new heart. Through those two projects I started to discover what made me who I was and to confront and deal with the abuse I had suffered as a child. I spent my days working on these projects and going to hospital appointments. After both heart attacks I did the Cardiac Rehabilitation Programme in the clinic in Dun Laoghaire and I continued to go there every week for blood tests. They monitored my blood pressure, heart rate, and the fluid in my lungs. If I put on two kilos in weight it could mean there was fluid in my lungs and I would be straight into hospital. I set up a little routine to distract myself.

My mobile phone was constantly with me; it was crucial that I knew where it was at all times. If a donor heart became available I had to be instantly contactable, as I had to be in the hospital within a half hour of getting the call. Zeta regularly made test calls to me and I always failed.

I was either driving, and not able to answer the phone, or I was on another call. I always called her back minutes later, but of course she was never one bit impressed with me. She drummed into me that it was vital I answered the phone, so I was very conscious of that, and got better at it.

As the days turned into weeks and the weeks turned into months I got weaker. I began to fear that I was not going to get a donor heart in time. I was waiting for something to happen; to get that phone call telling me there was a donor heart, but I didn't know if it was ever going to come. I was terrified that I was going to die. Another fear I had was that my health would get so bad and my heart would deteriorate to an extent that I would have to be hospitalised. I couldn't cope with the idea of being confined to a hospital bed. There was one man on the transplant waiting list at the same time as me who couldn't leave the hospital. He had a permanent IV with medication that was keeping him alive, so he couldn't go home. He was in hospital for over a year waiting for a donor organ. I was petrified that was going to happen to me.

Even though I hoped and prayed every day that I would get a donor heart, I was also afraid of having to undergo such major surgery. To hold the fear at bay I tried to keep myself busy doing something that was very important to me. I couldn't face my fear so I threw myself into doing media interviews. I became involved with donor awareness, which I feel very strongly about. I wanted to help as much as I could. I went on Joe Duffy to tell my story, hoping it would encourage people to carry donor cards and speak to their families about what they wanted to happen with their organs when they died.

I did a lot of interviews during Organ Donor Awareness Week.

There were only four heat transplants carried out in Ireland the year I went on the donor list and six the year after. It became my mission to raise awareness about the need for people to carry donor cards. I wanted to help in any way I could. I appeared on *The Late Late Show* on Good Friday 2011. Afterwards, when I was reflecting on the interview, I realised I was not emotionally or spiritually prepared for the transplant and I could no longer hide from how I was feeling. I had a lot of fear. But I was pretending to everybody around me and to myself that I was fine. I was doing what I always did, hiding behind a façade, the old restaurant manager persona, the showman that put a smile on his face; convincing myself and everyone else I was coping with what I was going through when I wasn't. I was running around doing interviews but what I was really doing was distracting myself from what was really happening and suppressing my fear.

Maria identified how scared I was and suggested I go see a counsellor to help me get through what was happening, and I agreed. I went to a counsellor who was one of the first to work with men in the Rape Crisis Centre and had helped a lot of abused men. I knew I was in the right place the minute I met her at my first session. She helped me deal with waiting for a heart transplant and prepared me for the procedure. I also spoke to her about the abuse I experienced during my childhood and she helped me face what had happened to me.

Working was simply not an option as I was not strong enough, so I had no income except for the illness benefit of €188 a week. I was struggling financially, which was causing more stress for me on top of trying to deal with waiting to get a donor heart and focusing on keeping myself as healthy as I could. I was out for lunch in Pichet with Elaine one day and the owner, Nick Munier, asked me how I was surviving financially and I admitted to him I was in serious trouble. He decided he was going to have a fundraising lunch for me. Four weeks later I was surrounded by friends and family who had all turned up to the event to support me. There were tables with people I went to college with, chefs and restaurant managers from all over Dublin. It was overwhelming to see so many people who I had worked and played with over the years coming to this lunch to help me. I was honoured. It was very emotional to feel the love and respect in that room. Ray Byrne and Jane English, the owners of the Wineport Lodge where *The Restaurant* was filmed, also held a fundraising lunch, and the money was divided between myself, the Irish Heart Foundation and the Irish Kidney Association. Those two events enabled me to continue my work with donor awareness and to live – not an extravagant life – just pay my bills, put food in my fridge and put petrol in my car. They had taken away the financial stress and worry I was carrying on top of everything else, which was such a relief.

The executive director of Vision Independent Productions, Philip Kamp, was eager to record another series of *The Restaurant* but was concerned I was not well enough to take part. He approached me with the idea of doing the show and I was really eager to be involved. I liked the idea of doing something I had loved doing before I was placed on the transplant list. When I asked my doctors if it was possible, they told me I was not to overdo things under any circumstances. I agreed to limited filming and really enjoyed it. But I was very different to the hyper maître d' who had previously been running around the set chatting to the celebrity chefs, the rest of the team and the audience. I was so weak I had to get into bed to rest, get up when I was required to do my piece on camera and then get straight back into bed. The directors worked around me, which was amazing. Everyone made sure my health came first.

People were so good to me, rallying around making sure they were there for me. I was astonished at the letters and texts of encouragement I received from people I had not met in years and members of the public I didn't even know. Those messages kept me going when I was struggling to stay positive. But as the time dragged on, it got more and more difficult for me to remain that way. The possibility that there was never going to be a donor heart for me, and that I could die, became more real. I was paralysed with fear. I needed to get out of Dublin and clear my head. I needed to escape my surroundings; give myself some time to breathe and calm myself. I was not meant to leave the city as I needed to be close to the hospital in case I got the call. But I felt like my apartment was closing in on me and I needed to get away somewhere that I could be alone with my thoughts. I needed open spaces to settle my racing mind and growing anxiety.

It was the June bank holiday and I got into my jeep and drove to Doonbeg in Clare. I stayed in a cottage and spent three days on my own taking long walks on the beach and driving through the Burren. It was wonderful to have fresh air, space and quiet time to myself. There was so much going on in Dublin and I was constantly surrounded by people who, with the best intentions, were giving me advice and telling me what

I should be doing. The Irish are great at thinking they know what is best for someone else. I took onboard the knowledge and expert advice from the medics and let that guide me to what felt right for me. There is a real primal earthiness and spirituality in the west of Ireland that is very special and exactly what I needed. I had my days alone getting comfortable with my challenging present and the obstacles I would face in the future.

I spent my evenings with my good friends Wade Murphy, a chef, and his wife Elaine who lived in Clare. We went to lovely restaurants and enjoyed good food and conversation. I had the perfect combination of time to myself and the company of good friends. My family from Toronto, on the Healy side, were visiting Ireland at the time and had rented a castle in Clare for a big reunion. After my couple of days getting away from everything I went to meet them all for the family reunion. As we sat around a table, I wondered if I would ever see so many members of my family together again. It was rare to have such a big family gathering and it was very emotional to think I might not be here to see it again. I had a real sense of my own mortality. It made me appreciate the experience even more and I spent the night talking and laughing with all my relatives. It was wonderful.

One day in October, I was sitting in my apartment alone, worrying whether I was ever going to be told there was a donor heart for me, when I got the call I had been waiting for. My mobile started ringing and Zeta's name was flashing on the monitor of the phone. Each time Zeta called everything went into slow motion. This time it was not a test call. She calmly told me they had a heart. I couldn't believe it; it was finally actually happening. I had imagined this moment for so long. I felt panic, excitement and fear, in that order. I automatically went into practical mode and made sure everything I needed was in my bag. I had gone over the drill in my head so many times, I knew exactly what I had to do.

Then, just as I was about to leave my apartment, the phone rang again. It was Zita. The donor heart was not suitable. I was crushed. The disappointment washed over me and I sank into my armchair and sat there in a daze, not sure what to do next. Thank God Zeta called me back and we had a long talk about what had just happened and how I was feeling.

I was getting very impatient. I had been on the transplant list for a year and I was beginning to think it was not going to happen in time. It felt as though time was running out and I was frightened. I knew that if my heart deteriorated much more, everything was going to become very difficult. I was getting weaker and I was terrified that I would soon be in hospital permanently, waiting for a donor heart, or dead. My biggest fears were now becoming reality. A week before Christmas I got another phone call from Zita. She told me there was a heart available and that they were sending an ambulance to my home to get me. I sat in the ambulance as it weaved in and out of the festive rush-hour traffic and I was very nervous, but also strangely calm.

When I arrived at the hospital I underwent a series of tests to see if I was compatible with the donor heart and if I was well enough to undergo the surgery. They carried out blood tests, a chest X-ray and checked my fluids, before shaving and scrubbing me in preparation for surgery. I was on the third floor of Celia's Ward for hours waiting to hear if today was the day. I spent a lot of time thinking about the person that had died – the donor – and what his or her family was going through. I also thought about the other person down the hall, in the same position as me, waiting to hear if they were going to be the recipient of the new heart. I prayed as I waited anxiously. I had visualised this happening so often that I felt ready. The documentary crew was with me in the hospital, recording my wait.

At 11.20 PM the doctor walked into my ward. I couldn't speak as I sat there staring at him, hoping he was going to tell me I was going to theatre. However, I was given the devastating news that the heart was going to the other patient. It was not happening for me tonight. There was a heart, but I couldn't have it. I was so close to having the transplant. I had prayed for so long and I was being told again it couldn't happen. I was not suitable for the heart transplant as the creatinine levels in my kidneys were way too high. I had been limping for a couple of weeks and thought I had twisted my ankle, so I was taking Ibuprofen to ease the pain. I didn't realise I was actually suffering from mild gout due to an increase in the level of uric acid in my body. Taking Ibuprofen is very bad for your kidneys when you're in a delicate state like I was, and it had put pressure on my kidneys, which increased my creatinine levels.

After I was told I was going home instead of getting a transplant, I simply got out of bed, got dressed, wished the nurses a Happy Christmas and walked out of the hospital. The staff in the hospital had tried to prepare me as best they could for a rejection. But you cannot understand the extent of your emotional response until it happens. As it turned out, the other person waiting for a heart was brought down to surgery and put under general anaesthetic, but then the donor heart went into cardiac arrest and was no longer useable. When the poor man regained consciousness he was told he'd never had the transplant.

It was Christmas so I was able to distract myself from my disappointment and growing fear. I went to my parents' house for Christmas and the family tried to keep things as normal as they could. I threw myself as best I could into the festive traditions. I was very weak but I tried my best to remain positive. It was not until the middle of January that everything really hit me and I fell apart. I crumbled onto the floor of my apartment and cried like a child for hours. It was like somebody turned on a tap, and once the tears started flowing they wouldn't stop. I was very angry, I felt very sorry for myself and I wanted it all to end. I couldn't stand it any more. I cried myself to sleep. For the next two weeks, I struggled to cope with everything; it was the toughest period I went through while on the waiting list. I didn't know whether I wanted to get up or stay in bed, I didn't know what I wanted to eat, whether I was coming or going.

I finally pulled myself out of that dark hole and once again became positive about my future, despite how bleak it looked. I tried to keep myself busy and started up a company called Zucchini Catering, which does food for the members' club in the O2. I set it up for somebody else but I did consultancy and worked there on occasion. People thought I was mad and I was doing too much but I had to keep my mind active.

One evening, I offered to mind my neighbour Cliona's children until her husband Darragh came back from work so that she could go out training with a running club. However, he arrived home early and she rang me to let me know I didn't need to watch the kids, but I popped up to see them anyway. Darragh had made spaghetti Bolognese for the kids' tea and offered me a bowl of it, which I jumped at. I was sitting there enjoying my meal and a chat with Darragh when, at 7.30 PM, my phone rang. It was Zita's name coming up on the monitor. I don't know why, but this time I knew this was it, I knew I was going to get a heart transplant. I jumped up out of my seat and ran out of my neighbour's apartment, shouting out as I left that this was *the* phone call. I told Zita I would meet the ambulance outside my apartment block and then rang my family and the director of the documentary to tell them it was happening. But the director was in Prague, so I told my friend who lived with me at the time, Mark O'Neill, who was a camera man, that he was going to have to record my journey to the hospital. I grabbed my bag, which had been packed and sitting at my bedroom door for over a year, and got into the ambulance. I was very excited; there was no fear this time.

I was in the hospital by 8 PM. I went straight up to the ward. I knew exactly what to do and what was going to happen; the experience at Christmas was a dress rehearsal. I went through all the tests again and was prepared for surgery. By 10 PM everything had calmed down and I knew I had hours of sitting in silence waiting to hear if I was finally going to get my transplant. I prayed and then rang my mother. She was so calm and asked me if I was afraid; I told her I wasn't and she reassured me everything was going to be fine. I asked her to say two prayers and light two candles – one for me and one for the donor.

It was 4.10 AM – over eight hours after I had been rushed to hospital

– when I heard Zita's footsteps coming down the corridor towards my room. She told the camera crew she was going to tell me now and I still didn't know. She sat down beside my bed. I can usually read somebody's face or their body language, but I couldn't figure out whether she was going to tell me I was finally getting a heart transplant or I was going home without one again. It seemed like the longest few seconds of my life just staring at her, waiting for her to speak. She looked me straight in the eyes and calmly told me the heart was mine; the operation was going ahead. Emotion welled up from within me and the tears started falling. It was going to happen, I was so relieved.

From that moment everything happened very quickly; there was no time to waste. I was in theatre within fifteen minutes. Zita walked beside me as I was wheeled towards the theatre. As I lay on the trolley outside the door of the theatre I could see doctors and nurses rushing around. Suddenly this dreadful fear took hold of me. I realised that the transplant was really going to happen; I was going to get a new heart. Images of the operation flashed before my eyes. I looked at Zita for reassurance. She took my hand and told me I was going to be fine. I believed her. It was out of my hands now; I had no control, so I started to relax. What will be, will be, I thought. In the anaesthetic room there was a big clock on the wall that read 4.25 AM. All the medics around me were chirpy and excited because a transplant was going ahead. A nurse told me I was going to be put under. I simply replied, 'In your own time darling, bless you all.' I looked down, and the last thing I remember was one of the nurse's clogs, which had little pink pigs on them, and then I fell asleep.

12

The Transplant

The best is yet to come.

The first forty-eight hours after a heart transplant are the most critical. It was 8.30 AM on Wednesday morning when I came out of theatre after four and a half hours in surgery. The next day I started to become aware of people and sounds around me, but nothing seemed real, it was like I was underwater or in an alternative universe. I was slipping in and out of consciousness. I was aware of the ICU surgical team and nurses around me; I could hear them but my eyes wouldn't open. As I drifted in and out, I was aware of them giving each other instructions and updating each other on my progress. They sounded like they were far away but I knew they were completely in control and so knowledgeable about what was going on, so much so that I let myself relax completely. Hearing them instilled confidence in me. I trusted them. I was lying in bed helpless, but I felt safe. They constantly carried out tests to ensure my body was not rejecting the donor heart. One of the cardiac surgical team, a woman called Tara softly told me that I was alright and the surgery had been a success. Those words registered with me. I had my heart. She came into my room every couple of hours to check on me and ask me how I felt and if I was in pain. To me it felt like she was asking me the same questions every five minutes, as I was floating between consciousness and unconsciousness. After I came around she told me that even in that state, after life-threatening surgery, my cheeky personality still shone through as my response every time was that the morphine was fabulous.

When I opened my eyes and became completely aware of my surroundings, I was lying in a white room. For a moment I was not sure if I was alive or dead. Once I registered where I was the first thing I did was slowly put my hands on my chest where my old, broken heart had once been. My chest felt foreign to me, like it was not part of my body, but a piece of armour. I wanted to feel what had happened to my body and how my life had been saved by my donor and the doctors. My chest was bandaged up but I could feel the ridge where I had been cut open and where my bone had been separated and was now being held together. The magnitude of what I had gone through and the incredible gift I had been given by my donor washed over me in a wave of gratitude and amazement.

It was very sore, but it was surreal to realise the heart transplant I had prayed and hoped to get for sixteen months had finally happened. My stomach was also bandaged and completely swollen and I was attached to lots of tubes and machines. I started to become aware of my circulation, my blood pounding through my body at a speed I wasn't used to. I could feel it reaching the very tips of my fingers and my toes, which it had not done since I had become ill. It was like a fast-flowing river rushing though me. There was vitality in my body that I had not experienced in a long time. I knew how sick I had been, but the sensations pulsing through my body really made me realise the extent to which my body had been weakened. I was amazed at how I could feel the benefits of having a new heart immediately. I felt like it was still my body, but newer and fresher. My hair and skin felt healthier. Even my teeth felt revitalised. As I lay in that bed, sore and stiff, I still knew I had been given a new lease of life. It was like a new energy and life source flowing through my entire body. I was relieved and overcome with joy at what was happening to me.

My mum and my sister Mary came in to see me on Friday morning. It was clear how much everything had taken out of them when I saw the relief on their exhausted faces. My father had been taken into hospital that morning with a minor stomach upset. They had so much to worry about, but when they saw me awake they just looked at me and smiled. They had come so close to losing me but they maintained a brave front, always remaining positive and strong for me. I was so happy to see them. There was no need for words; they came and held my hands and the tears ran freely down our faces. It was a moment I had dreamt of since the day I went on the donor transplant list.

I was very weak. I got tired often and slept a lot. There was a nurse with me throughout the day and night. If I needed anything, there was always someone there to help me. I let them take care of me and do what they had to do to help make me more comfortable. They were all so happy and full of joy to be part of this experience; this miracle happening. Their amazing care was integral to my recovery. I was content to lie still and allow my body to do whatever it needed to replenish and rebuild with my new heart.

The physiotherapist Irene Byrne was a joy to be around. The positive energy she gave me was phenomenal. On Friday evening she came to see me and told me it was time to get out of bed, as far as the chair beside it. Irene told me that by the following Monday I would be standing again and by Wednesday I would be walking. Considering how I felt physically I didn't believe her, but I was prepared to do anything I was told to do. I trusted all the hospital staff completely. And come Monday I was on my feet again. Standing up for the first time after my heart transplant was like being reborn. I was like a baby learning how to do everything again; things I had taken for granted, like standing up and walking, my new body had to re-learn.

When I was first helped out of bed I was crouched over and Irene told me to stand taller and put my head up, which I did. Slowly and gradually I got bigger and taller. I was sore, but I felt amazing, in awe and completely alive. It was like re-entering the world. Every day I did something new and got stronger. Gradually I started walking. It was a painstaking process, just a couple of steps at a time. I was carrying ten kilograms of additional fluid in my body, which made it even more difficult. But everything Irene asked me to do I did to the best of my ability.

I also slowly began to start eating again. The only thing I craved was my favourite snack for years, a toasted ham and cheese sandwich. I told a woman in the catering section of the hospital about my longing for one but there were no sandwich toaster in the kitchen to make it. But that wonderful woman appeared one day with a toasted sandwich for me. I don't know how she did it, but it was one of the tastiest I had ever eaten. I knew my road to recovery was going to be a long one but as I munched on that snack I knew I was on the right path. I felt almost euphoric, which was probably assisted by the high quantity of medication.

I was given limited access to my mobile phone and got immense encouragement from the hundreds of text messages from friends, colleagues and family. News of my heart transplant also spread on Facebook and Twitter and the words of support were amazing. I was excited about the prospect of getting to a place where I could lead a healthy life, but I was also happy to take things slowly and get there gradually. I felt like I was in the middle of a finale after a long-running show. I had been through so much; suffering two heart attacks and waiting sixteen months for a transplant and now I was coming to the end of that particular part of my life.

The Intensive Care Unit in the Mater Hospital became the perfect cocoon in which to heal, protected from the outside world. The nurses were so fantastic, kind and caring. They made me feel like I was a part of their family, and I suppose I *was* part of a family in the ICU, where I had to be cared for like a child. There were many nights when I was not able to sleep with thoughts racing though my head of what I had been through; how lucky I was to be alive and gratitude to my donor. But I was never left lying there alone. There was always a nurse willing to listen and talk to me. I often lay chatting to a nurse in the early hours of the morning, suggesting recipes for buffets and dishes for family occasions and recommending the best restaurants. One nurse, Vanessa, was getting married eight weeks later and we spent hours talking about her wedding plans and the little touches that would make her reception extraordinary. I was surrounded by wonderful people. It was a very special place to be, the perfect environment for healing. I will always have fond memories of ICU. It was the beginning of the rest of my life with my new heart.

A biopsy was carried out to check if my new heart and the tissue around it were being accepted by my body. The test is rated from zero to five; with five the most acute rejection and zero the least level of rejection. I was overjoyed when Dr Jim McCarthy told me my results came back at level one. He informed me they were very pleased with the transplant and the progress I was making. Everything was going swimmingly and I couldn't have been happier. I was moved to the High Dependency Ward when I got a bit stronger. It was another little step in my recovery.

The care I got was out of this world. I was in awe of the dedication of the medical staff. I felt more relaxed there as I had my own room. When they took the tubes and drains out of me I had a little bit more freedom – I was able to get out of bed and put on my own clothes. I started to feel more and more like my old self, but with a healthy heart. I was in no rush to go anywhere and was prepared to take my recovery very slowly. I appreciated every small bit of progress I made.

My family were the only ones allowed to visit me, to ensure I didn't get any infections and I was in semi-isolation due to the immune suppression drugs. When visiting regulations were relaxed I started arranging for close friends to come to the hospital to see me. My mobile phone was banned, apart from occasional exceptions The nurses were right to do that, but I was missing hearing about what was going on in Dublin and what was happening in my friends' lives. I wanted to hear the juicy gossip and was eager to be filled in on what I was missing. It was wonderful catching up with my dearest friends; I loved hearing all the news. That was a real sign that I was getting better.

The whole time I was in the hospital after the heart transplant I lay semi-upright with my arms across my chest. I was protecting my new heart. I felt a strong spiritual connection with my donor. I have great respect for this person's heart and I wanted to make sure I didn't break it or hurt it. I became very in tune with myself and embraced a true sense of spirituality. I felt a real connection with my maker, with God. It was like both God and my donor were with me the whole time, encouraging and helping me. I felt their presence. I had conversations with them every day. The minute I opened my eyes every morning the first thing I did was thank my donor for the most wonderful gift anyone could be given: the gift of life. I was alive because of him. I also thanked God for helping me get to this point and for my heart being accepted into my body.

I have always been mindful that the reason I am alive is that somebody tragically passed away. One Sunday the doctors agreed to let me leave my ward and go to the church in the hospital. I had not been at Mass for years, but I needed to be somewhere that I could sit in silence with a spiritual presence surrounding me. I didn't want to attend a service, listen to a homily or speak to a priest. I just wanted to be there. I lit a candle in memory of my donor and another one for his family.

Despite my elation at the prospect of full recovery, during my time in hospital I experienced a rollercoaster of emotions. I went from euphoria to depression and anxiety. I often found myself crying with joy and sadness at the same time. It is an amazing, privileged experience. It is a unique journey that only people who have experienced a transplant can truly understand. The following Sunday I was walking down the hospital corridor chatting away to my mother when out of nowhere this huge wave of emotion washed over me. Mid-sentence I just came to a standstill and the tears started rolling down my face. My poor mother was standing there, not quite sure what was wrong with me or what she should do. It had hit me that the waiting was finally over. I had been sick for five years and I had lived with a phone in my hand for sixteen months, waiting for that call. It was such a relief to finally be standing there with my new heart. A weight had been lifted off me and I felt such relief and a sense of closure. When Dr McCarthy removed my old heart he took with it all the pain of the past. As I stood there crying I felt a sense of peace, it was a moment of clarity. I had discovered how to live in the moment, rather than being haunted by the past or fretting about the future. I was in no rush to leave the hospital, I had the patience to let myself recover at the pace my body needed.

After two weeks and two days the medical team decided I was strong enough to go home. I was given a bag of medication and a list of strict rules I had to obey to make sure I protected myself from infection. Walking out the hospital door was terrifying. I left the cocooned safety of the sterile hospital full of medical experts who knew how best to care for me and entered a society full of noise and bacteria that could jeopardise my recovery. Going back into the big, bad world was like jumping into a vast ocean. While in hospital, surrounded by medics, I foolishly thought that I was strong enough to cope in my own apartment. But when it came time to leave I realised how much I needed my family. I felt vulnerable and needed to be protected, so I went to the same place I have gone throughout my life when I needed help: my parents' home. They have always been my constant source of support and love. My mother went to great lengths to clean her already spotless house for my arrival. She even shampooed the carpets in preparation for my homecoming.

It was crucial I didn't pick up an infection. The main rule was no kissing, no animals and no children. I will never forget the look on my parents' faces when I walked through their front door. They just stood there looking at me with relief and pure love in their eyes. Their only son was home with a healthy heart and a future.

Every morning my father brought me breakfast on a tray: a bowl of porridge, brown bread toasted and boiled eggs. It was my mother that tentatively opened my bedroom door to deliver healthy lunches and dinners that only a mother can cook. They nursed me back to health. That first weekend I went only from the bed to the bathroom and maybe to the sofa. I was exhausted. But I was so appreciative I was still alive that even being able to do that was great. I had been given a second chance at life and I was going to do my utmost to make sure I became the healthy, contented person I knew I could be. After a couple of days I found the strength around midday to get out of bed and get dressed. I loved going for short walks or chatting with my mother in the kitchen over a cup of tea. The things I had once taken for granted became the most important part of my day. It was like seeing the world through new eyes. I appreciated the simple, everyday things that really matter. I was happy to give my body time to regenerate and recuperate from the trauma it had been through. I knew I was going to be alright. I kept my mobile turned off – which was an extremely difficult thing for me to do. I was itching to know what was going on with my friends. But I knew that it was necessary to take time out and look after myself. My priority was me, my health, and taking care of the heart I was so blessed to have been given. I didn't even tell anyone but my family and a handful of close friends I was out of hospital It was liberating to give myself ten days to recover and heal. Disappearing to my parents' house without people knowing was the best thing I could have done. I had silence, with no demands, surrounded by people that loved me and looked after me. I didn't have to be the constantly entertaining, funny guy with the witty one-liners, or the attentive maître d' who made people feel special. It was now time for me to look after myself. It took two heart attacks and a heart transplant to realise that. Now I knew what was important.

However, once I felt strong enough I wanted to be back in Dublin, surrounded by my friends, who are like a second family to me. My flatmate at the time, Mark, cleaned the apartment to the point that I hardly recognised the place. There was no clutter; not a speck of dust. But it was not sterile; the books I had read were still on the shelves, the framed photographs capturing wonderful memories were still everywhere and the paintings I had bought on my travels were still hanging on the wall. It was home. It was lovely to be back in my own apartment.

My friends rallied around me and I was never left on my own. There was always someone there making sure I had everything I needed. They did my shopping and made sure my fridge was always full – of healthy food of course! They went to the pharmacy to get my long list of medication and cooked me dinners, ensuring my strict dietary requirements were met. I had been told by the doctors before I left the hospital that I was not to eat anything that was not cooked or peeled, which meant I was not allowed many foods that I adored. There was no blue vein cheese, shellfish, or smoked salmon. Initially I couldn't eat fruit or salads either. I could not eat anything raw as my immune system was so weak. Any bacteria could set me back or cause an infection so I had to be very careful.

I also had to stay away from animals and small children because they carry infection and bacteria. Everyone that came near me had to clean their hands with hand sanitiser. Despite the restrictions I was never alone. I was not able to leave the house much but I always had someone to sit and have a natter with.

I told two of my friends I would love to have an exercise bike, as I had used one in hospital twice a day for ten minutes to improve my cardiovascular fitness. Within days there was one in my sitting room. I was not able to drive for ten weeks and there was always a friend willing to take me to my many hospital appointments. I felt safer in Dublin, as I was close to the hospital. Knowing I was only minutes away from medical help if I needed it put my mind at rest.

Gary, who has been one of my most constant, faithful friends, had booked flights to Ireland to visit me while I was on the transplant list, but by time he was due to arrive I was after undergoing the surgery. He was going to cancel the trip as he thought it might have been too much for me, but I was having none of it and insisted he come to see me. I was really happy to have him around me. He stayed in a hotel close to my apartment and every day he came to visit me. We spent hours talking about the past, the present and the future, that at times I had feared I may not make it. While I was recovering I divided my time between Dublin and Naas. I immersed myself in my life in Dublin and then took a little sabbatical in my parent's house. I spent three or four days in Dublin and then my father collected me and I went home for a couple of days.

Slowly I began to get stronger. The pain in my chest began to subside; I could feel my chest healing and knitting back together. My energy came back. I walked every day for half an hour, which was a wonderful thing to be able to do. I also did ten minutes each day on my exercise bike. I was now able to walk to the supermarket down the road without stopping for a break, which I couldn't do before the transplant. Being able to do the simple things in life, which most people take for granted, was a joy. I was very happy to be alive.

However, in June my energy began to get lower. I had been told to expect a lull, as I had been running on false energy from the euphoria of getting the transplant. I came back down to earth with a bang – everything became real again and it hit me hard. I started asking myself if I deserved this heart. I felt a huge responsibility to look after it. I became anxious and my emotions were all over the place. Some days I couldn't get out of bed and would stay there crying, not knowing why I was upset. I was scared.

Recognising my symptoms, I identified that I was depressed and addressed it. I went to a counsellor, which helped a lot. Physically I was fine, but psychologically I had to deal with what I had gone through. I knew I had to be patient and work through how I was feeling. I didn't want anybody around; I needed space to come to terms with what had happened. I made sure I got out of the house every day for a walk or to the shop. This depression lasted two months and was the most difficult part of my whole recovery. It finally lifted and I came out the other end. It was then that I saw the marvellous wonder of the world around me again and I felt great freedom. I started trying to decide what I was going to do with the rest of my life. It is like buying a new coat and trying on a few to see what fits. I had to become aware of what my body was capable of doing.

Every day is now a blessing. I have a new lease of life and live every day to the full. I love going on walks, out for meals with my friends and spending time with my family. I am busy working with Zucchini Catering, a new series of *The Restaurant* is in the pipeline, I am planning to set up a charity to raise funds for long-term heart patients in hospital, to give them the luxuries of home they miss, and doing as much as I can to raise awareness about transplants and urging people to carry donor cards. For the first time, my life has become very simple. I am living in the moment and it is marvellous. I am not dwelling on the past or worrying about the future. I have this sense of peace.

I am humbled, honoured and blessed that a person I never knew has given me this wonderful gift of a heart. This person saved my life. I feel like I knew him, even though I never met him. But in another time, in another place, I would have been honoured to call him my friend. He is part of me and not a day goes by that I don't think about him and his family. I have a strong spiritual connection with my donor. I feel his spirit with me all the time, which gives me great comfort. My prayers will always be offered for my donor and his family. I am so grateful to him for carrying a donor card.

I don't know what the future holds for me. But I do know I am ready to follow my new heart.